# BR'ER COTTON

## BY TEARRANCE ARVELLE CHISHOLM

*Br'er Cotton* was first performed in the UK at Theatre503, London,
on 12 March 2018.

*Br'er Cotton* was shortlisted for both the Theatre503 Playwriting Award 2016
and Relentless Award. *Br'er C___
Network Rolling World Prem___
Depth Ensemble Theater (Lo___
(Cleveland, OH) as ___

# BR'ER COTTON

## BY TEARRANCE ARVELLE CHISHOLM

### CAST

|  |  |
|--:|:--|
| **Ruffrino/Son** | Michael Ajao |
| **Nadine/Mother** | Kiza Deen |
| **Matthew/Grandfather** | Trevor A Toussaint |
| **Caged_Bird99** | Ellie Turner |
| **Officer** | Alexander Campbell |

### CREATIVE TEAM

|  |  |
|--:|:--|
| **Director** | Roy Alexander Weise |
| **Designer** | Jemima Robinson |
| **Lighting Designer** | Amy Mae |
| **Sound Designer** | Harry Johnson |
| **Video Designer** | Louise Rhoades-Brown |
| **Movement Director** | Vicki Manderson |
| **Assistant Director** | Jordan John |

### PRODUCTION TEAM

|  |  |
|--:|:--|
| **Producer** | Jake Orr |
| **Assistant Producer** | Samara Thomas |
| **Production Manager** | Ed Borgnis |
| **Stage Manager** | Tomos Derrick |
| **Assistant Stage Manager** | Ane Miren Arriaga |
| **Costume Supervisor** | Hanne Talbot |
| **PR** | Nancy Poole |

# CAST

**RUFFRINO/SON – MICHAEL AJAO**
Michael trained at the Brit School. Theatre includes: *The Lorax* (Old Vic); *Lord of the Flies* (Regent's Park Open Air Theatre national tour) and *Liberian Girl* (Royal Court Theatre).

Film includes: *Attack The Block* (Big Talk Pictures/Film 4).

Television includes: *Cuffs* (BBC).


**NADINE/MOTHER – KIZA DEEN**
Kiza trained at RADA. Theatre includes: *Trouble In Mind* (Bath Theatre Royal); *Expensive Sh\*t* (Soho Theatre); *Hamlet, As You Like It, All's Well That Ends Well* (Royal Shakespeare Company) and *Yard Gal* (RADA Festival).

Television includes: *Hollyoaks* (Channel 4) and *Silent Witness* (BBC).


**MATTHEW/GRANDFATHER – TREVOR A TOUSSAINT**
Theatre includes: *Guys and Dolls* (Royal Exchange Theatre, Manchester); *The Bubbly Black Girl Sheds Her Chameleon Skin* and *The Harder They Come* (Stratford East Theatre Royal); *Screamin' Jay Hawkins; 125th Street* (Shaftesbury Theatre); *Fences* (Duchess Theatre); *Les Blancs* (National Theatre); *Sister Act* (Gordon Craig Theatre); *Elegies for Angels, Punks and Raging Queens* (Bridewell Theatre); *Lost In The Stars* (Battersea Arts Centre); *An African Cargo* and *Ska Ba Day* (Talawa/Greenwich Theatre); *Wind in the Willows* and *Alice in Wonderland* (The Brewhouse); *A Day At The Racist* (Finborough Theatre); *The Threepenny Opera* (Pimlico Opera) and *Jungle Book* (Birimingham Stage Company national tour).

Television includes: *Donald Pennington, Obsession,* and *Dark Desires* (October Films/ID Channel); *Marriage of Reason and Squalor* (Sky Arts); *VIP* (Running Bear/Channel 4); *Sinister Ministers* (Firecracker Films/ID Channel); *Crisis Control* (CBBC) and *Sofia's Diary* (Fouth Passenger/Channel 5).

Film includes: *Street Boy* (Lokum Productions); *Support* (Scoop Films/GilliesWorks); *Life Sentence* (Urban Way Productions); *Meat* (Mustard Productions) and *London Fields* (Muses Productions).


**CAGED_BIRD99 – ELLIE TURNER**
Theatre includes: *Orca* (Southwark Playhouse); *R and D* (Hampstead Theatre); *Stone Face, Merit* and *Drama At Inish* (Finborough Theatre); *Nordost* (Salisbury Playhouse/ Theatre Royal Bath); *Hamlet, The Cherry Orchard* and *Hamlet* (National Theatre); *Bloody Poetry* (The White Bear); *The School for Wives* (Upstairs at the Gatehouse Theatre); *Oliver Twist* (Riverside Studios/UK tour); *Avocado* (Osip/The King's Head Theatre); *La Ronde* (Riverside Studios); *Alphabetical Order* (The Mill at Sonning); *The Playboy of the Western World* and *Henry V* (Riverside Studios/UK tour).

Television includes: *The Stuarts – A Bloody Reign* (3DD Productions) and *Misfits* (Clerkenwell Films for E4).

Film includes: *Jungle Book* (The Imaginarium Studios/Warner Bros); *If You Can Hear Me* (Fuel TV); *Science* (Aether Production/JustFilms); *How You Look At Me* (TTOU Ltd); *Black Cab* (Twenty One Productions) and *TV Audioville* (Mark Tintner).

Awards include: Ian Charleston Commendations for *Hindle Wakes* and *The School for Wives.* Best Actress for *Black Cab* at the Golden Egg Film Festival, NYC.

**OFFICER – ALEXANDER CAMPBELL**
Alexander trained at Arts Educational School. Theatre includes: *The Revenger's Tragedy* (Nottingham Playhouse); *Serpent's Tooth* (Almeida Theatre); *One Flew Over the Cuckoo's Nest* (Curve Theatre); *Three Musketeers and The Princess of Spain* (English Touring Theatre); *Prodigal Son* (Stephen Joseph Theatre); *Merlin & The Cave of Dreams* (Manchester Library); *Six Degrees of Separation* (Royal Exchange Theatre, Manchester); *Antigone* (Jerwood Space); *The Boys Next Door* (Tabard Theatre).

Television includes: *Maigret*, *Lucan* and *Murder Investigation Team* (ITV); *The Bill* (Thames Television) and *Casualty* (BBC).

Awards include: The Stage 'Best Solo Performer' Nomination for *Private Peaceful* and Manchester Evening News Award for *Private Peaceful*.

# CREATIVE TEAM

### PLAYWRIGHT – TEARRANCE ARVELLE CHISHOLM

Tearrance's play *Br'er Cotton* is in the middle of its American Rolling World Premiere through the National New Play Network, with productions at Kitchen Dog Theater in Dallas, Lower Depth Ensemble Theater in Los Angeles and Cleveland Public Theater. Tearrance also recently participated in the Magic Theater's Virgin Play Festival with a workshop presentation of his newest play, *PYG.*

Previous productions: *Hooded: Or Being Black for Dummies* at Mosaic Theater in DC (Helen Hayes Nomination: Charles MacArthur Award for Outstanding Original New Play or Musical), *Br'er Cotton* (The Catholic University of America), *Bhavi the Avenger* (Convergence Theatre), *In Sweet Remembrance* (Endstation Theatre Company) and *A Month of Sundays* (Midwinter Madness Short Play Festival). He has developed new works with Signature Theatre, Theatre J, Theatre Alliance, The Kennedy Center American College Theatre Festival and has held residencies at The Bay Area Playwrights Festival, The Virginia Center for Creative Arts, Djerassi Resident Artists Program and The Eugene O'Neill National Playwrights Conference. He was a finalist for the inaugural Relentless Award and the Theatre503 Playwriting Award. Tearrance received two of the 2016 National KCACTF awards, the Rosa Parks Playwriting Award and the Lorraine Hansberry Playwriting Award. Tearrance was a part of the Pacific Playwrights Festival at South Coast Rep with his play *Anacostia Street Lions*. He developed the play *Black Lady Authority* under the auspices of the Sundance Theater Lab. Tearrance holds an MFA in Playwriting from the Catholic University of America. He is currently in the Lila Acheson Wallace American Playwrights Program at Julliard, and is a Sundance Institute and Time Warner Foundation Fellow, and a 2050 Fellow at New York Theater Workshop.

### DIRECTOR – ROY ALEXANDER WEISE

Roy Alexander Weise is the 19th annual winner of the James Menzies-Kitchin Award and directed his critically acclaimed, sell-out production of *The Mountaintop* by Katori Hall at the Young Vic.

Current and forthcoming productions include: *Nine Night* (National Theatre).

Theatre includes: *Jekyll and Hyde* (National Youth Theatre); *Dead Don't Floss* (National Theatre); *The Ugly One* (Park Theatre, Buckland Theatre Company); *The Dark* (Fuel/Ovalhouse); *Zero for the Young Dudes* (Young & Talented in association with NT Connections); *The Mountaintop* (Young Vic); *Primetime* (Royal Court); *Stone Face* (Finborough Theatre).

Assistant Director credits include: *Hangmen* (Royal Court/West End); *X, Escaped Alone, You For Me For You, Primetime 2015, Violence and Son, Who Cares* and *Liberian Girl* (Royal Court); *Albion* and *We Are Proud To Present...* (Bush Theatre); *The Serpent's Tooth* (Talawa/Almeida Theatre).

For television, Roy was Trainee Director on *Invisible* (Red Room/Ballet Boys/Channel 4).

Roy has previously worked at the Royal Court as the Trainee Director, at the Bush Theatre and Lyric Hammersmith as the BBC Theatre Fellow and at The Red Room as Associate Artist.

Roy is now Associate Director at the Harts Theatre Company and Lead Acting Tutor at Young & Talented School of Stage & Screen.

## DESIGNER – JEMIMA ROBINSON

Jemima is the current recipient of the Max Rayne Design Bursary Award at the National Theatre. Jemima is the winner of the biennial Linbury Prize for Stage Design and the Bristol Old Vic Technical Theatre Award in 2011. She is a former resident artist at Kenya's Kuona Arts Trust in Nairobi and resident designer for Istanbul's Talimhane Theatre.

Theatre includes: *The Majority* (National Theatre); *New Nigerians*, *Thebes Land* (nominated for Best Set Design and winner of Best Production, Offie Awards); *Maria de Buenos Aires* (Arcola Theatre); *Parallel Yerma* (Young Vic); *License to Ill* and *This Will End Badly* (Southwark Playhouse); *Biedermann and the Arsonists* (winner of the Independent Opera Award, Sadler's Wells); *Mapping Brent* (Tricycle Theatre); *The Dark Room* (Theatre503); *Dyl* and *Sparks* (Old Red Lion Theatre) and *Hearing Things* (Albany Theatre).

## LIGHTING DESIGNER – AMY MAE

Amy trained at RADA on the postgraduate Stage Electrics and Lighting Design course and has a degree in Stage Management and Performing Arts from the University of Winchester and works across theatre, dance, site specific and devised performance. Amy designed the lighting for the acclaimed 'Pie Shop' version of *Sweeney Todd: The Demon Barber of Fleetstreet*, which is currently playing at the Barrow Street Theatre in New York. She won the Knight of Illumination Award in 2016 for the London production, and her designs for the New York production have been nominated for the 2017 Drama Desk Award for Outstanding Lighting Design and the Lucille Lortel Award for Best Lighting.

Upcoming credits include: *Mountains: The Dreams of Lily Kwok* (Royal Exchange Theatre, Manchester).

Theatre includes: *Othello*, *Jekyll and Hyde* and *The Host* (NYT Rep Season 2017); *Half Breed* (Talawa/Soho Theatre & Assembly Rooms); *Start Swimming* (Young Vic/ Summerhall Edinburgh); *The Ugly One* (Park Theatre); *Babette's Feast* (The Print Room); *The Lounge* (Soho Theatre); *Wordsworth* (Theatre by the Lake); *Paradise of the Assassins* (Tara Theatre); *Knife Edge* (Pond Restaurant, Dalston); *Minaturists 55* (Arcola Theatre); *Prize Fights* (Royal Academy of Dramatic Art); *Orphans* (Southwark Playhouse); *Macbeth* (Italia Conti); *I'm Not Here Right Now* (Paines Plough's Roundabout/Soho Theatre); *Liolà* (New Diorama Theatre); *Children in Uniform* and *Punk Rock* (Tristan Bates Theatre); *Sweeney Todd* (Harringtons Pie and Mash Shop/West End); *The Three Sisters* (Cockpit Theatre); *Cat Couture* (Music Video); *In Bed* (London Theatre Workshop); *Henry V* (Royal Academy of Dramatic Art); *Pool*, *The Gut Girls* (Brockley Jack Theatre) and *The Legacy* (The Place).

Programming includes: *Jeux* (Royal Opera House); *Tannhauser* (Longborough Festival Opera); *Robin Hood* (Stratford East Theatre Royal); *Lela & Co.* (Royal Court Theatre); *Dirty Butterfly* and *Red Forest* (The Young Vic).

Amy was one of the invited speakers at the 2017 Showlight Conference in Florence.

## SOUND DESIGNER – HARRY JOHNSON

Theatre includes: *The Secret Keeper* (Ovalhouse); *Jekyll & Hyde* (Ambassadors Theatre); *Babette's Feast* (Print Room Coronet); *Killing Time* and *The Gathered Leaves* (Park Theatre); *Boy with Beer* (King's Head Theatre); *Wolf Man* (Platform Studio Theatre) and *Woyzeck Theory* (Courtyard Theatre).

Theatre as Assistant Sound Designer includes: *Maladie de la Mort* (Théâtre des Bouffes du Nord); *Touch* (Soho Theatre); *City of Glass* (HOME/Lyric Hammersmith); *Oil* (Almeida Theatre) and *Schatten* (Schaubühne).

## VIDEO DESIGNER – LOUISE RHOADES-BROWN

Louise is a highly skilled Video & Projection Designer. She trained at Ravenbourne College. Her work can be seen across the UK and internationally.

Recent theatre, live events, and corporate work include: *Rothschild & Sons* (Park Theatre); *Immersive Show; Luv Esther/Part 2* (UK tour); *Legally Blonde* (Korea/Monte Carlo); *The Ugly One* and *The Trial of Jane Fonda* (Park Theatre); *A Thousand Faces, The Artificial Brain, Worst Wedding Ever* (Salisbury Playhouse); *Dracula* (Resorts World, Singapore); *The Island Nation* (Arcola Theatre); *Merch Yr Eog* (Theatre Genedlaethol, Cymru); *Bugsy Malone* (Leicester Curve); *Ray Mears: Tales of Endurance* (UK tour); *An Evening With Ray Mears* (UK tour); *Box of Photographs* (Polka Theatre); *Legally Blonde* (Leicester Curve); *Chwalfa* (Pontio); *Monster in the Maze* (Barbican); *Fugee & Wasted* and *Gods & Monsters* (Southwark Playhouse); *The Prodigals* (The Belgrade); *Fallujah* (The Cockpit); *The Handyman* (UK tour); *1936* (Lilian Baylis Theatre); *Romeo and Juliet* (Headlong/national tour); *Opera Holland Park* (Corporate Party); *Queen With Adam Lambert* (world tour); *Gravity Levity* (Research Project); *Josh Groban's Straight to You Tour* (multi-arena USA tour); *Procter & Gamble's Hairworld* (Paris); *Versus Versace spring/summer 16* (Content Manager); *Nokia, Internal Communications* (Internal Web Videos); *Promax* (Conference & Awards Graphics); *The Hate Game* (Holocaust Memorial Day).

As Associate Video Designer: *The End of Longing* (The Playhouse); *Alice's Adventures In Underground* (Waterloo Vaults); *Building Mapping* (Islington Square Festival of Culture); *Lord Attenborough Tribute* (The University of Sussex); *The Merchant of Venice* (Almedia Theatre); *Flashmob* (UK tour); *The Waterbabies* (Ed Curtis); *The Flying Dutchman* (English National Opera, London); *Raymond Gubby's Aida* (The Royal Albert Hall); *Pippin* (The Menier Chocolate Factory); *Reasons to be Cheerful* (Graeae/The New Wolsey Theatre).


## MOVEMENT DIRECTOR – VICKI MANDERSON

Movement Direction includes: *The Almighty Sometimes* (Royal Exchange Theatre, Manchester); *Cockpit* (Lyceum Edinburgh); *We're Still Here* (National Theatre Wales); *Jimmy's Hall* (Abbey Theatre); *306* (National Theatre of Scotland); *a profoundly affectionate, passionate devotion to someone – noun* (Royal Court Theatre); *See Me Now* (Young Vic); *The Tempest* (Beijing Xinchan); *Details* (Grid Iron); *Kidnapped* (RCS); *Housed* (Old Vic New Voices); *A Serious Case of The Fuckits, Loaded* and *I Do Believe in Monsters* (Royal Central School of Speech & Drama).

Associate Movement Director credits include: *The Twits* (Royal Court); *Let The Right One In* (National Theatre of Scotland/Royal Court/West End); *The Curious Incident of the Dog in the Night-Time* (National Theatre/West End); *Blackwatch, In Time of Strife* (National Theatre Scotland).


## ASSISTANT DIRECTOR – JORDAN JOHN

NYT member Jordan John is both a writer and performer, and a former Theatre503 Five-O-Fresh participant.

His upcoming work as a screenwriter will be *Lovebirds* and *Mornings are the Hardest*.

This is his first role as an assistant director and he is set to work with Wolab this coming March.

# PRODUCTION TEAM

### PRODUCER – JAKE ORR
Jake is the Producer at Theatre503.

Producing includes: *In Event of Moone Disaster* (Theatre503); *No Miracles Here* (Edinburgh Festival Fringe, The Lowry and Shoreditch Town Hall); *Gutted* (Edinburgh Festival Fringe/HOME); *BLUSH* (Edinburgh Festival Fringe/Soho Theatre/national tour); *Weald* (Finborough Theatre); *Shelter Me* (Theatre Delicatessen) and Incoming Festival (New Diorama, 2014–17).

Associate Producing includes: *Lists for the End of the World* (Edinburgh Festival Fringe); *The Bombing of the Grand Hotel* (Cockpit Theatre/Brighton Fringe); *Mouse Plague* (Edinburgh Festival Fringe/BAC/tour); *The Eradication of Schizophrenia in Western Lapland* (Edinburgh Festival Fringe/BAC/national and international tour).

Jake also founded A Younger Theatre and Incoming Festival and was nominated for Best Producer in the 2014 Off West End Awards.

### ASSISTANT PRODUCER – SAMARA THOMAS
Samara is currently the Resident Assistant Producer at Theatre503.

Producing includes: *Macbeth*, *Hansel and Gretel* (Iris Theatre). Samara also has experiences as Assistant Project Manager (Watford Palace Theatre) and as Arts Officer (African Caribbean Society) whilst studying for her Theatre BA at Brunel University.

### PRODUCTION MANAGER – ED BORGNIS
Ed is a Production Manager working in the UK and worldwide. Recent projects include: *Impossible* (Jamie Henry Productions/world tour); *Mozart Vs. Machine* (Mahogany); *Austentatious* (Underbelly/West End); *Cathy* (Cardboard Citizens); *Disco Pigs* (Tara Finney Productions); *Black and Gold* (Google/Roundhouse); a series of *Star Wars* launch events for HP and The Grand Journey European tour for Bombay Sapphire.

Ed has worked for the Sound departments of the Royal Shakespeare Company, Royal Ballet, Regent's Park Open Air Theatre, Shakespeare's Globe, Tricycle Theatre, and various concert venues. He also dabbles in video design and provides broadcast engineering support for the BBC.

Ed has a Postgraduate Engineering degree from University of Warwick and grew up in London and Norfolk.

### STAGE MANAGER – TOMOS DERRICK
Tomos trained at LAMDA.

Theatre includes: *The Moor* (Old Red Lion Theatre); *The Dark Room* and *Hyem* (Theatre503).

### ASSISTANT STAGE MANAGER – ANE MIREN ARRIAGA
Ane trained at CIFP Tartanga.

Stage Management includes: *The Words Are Coming Now* and *The Knitting Pattern* (Theatre503).

Assistant Stage Management includes: *Escape The Scaffold* and *Punts* (Theatre503).

**COSTUME SUPERVISOR – HANNE TALBOT**
Hanne trained at the Royal Central School of Speech and Drama.

Costume Supervision includes: *New Nigerians*, *Drones, Baby, Drones* and *Kenny Morgan* revival (Arcola Theatre); *Decades* (Ovalhouse); *A Flea In Her Ear* (Tabard Theatre); *Othello* (Smooth Faced Gentlemen).

Wardrobe Supervision includes: *Aladdin* (Imagine Theatre); *The Wipers Times* (Arts Theatre/UK tour); *All or Nothing: The Mod Musical* (The Vaults); *Pentecost* (Derby Live).

Hanne has assisted on productions including: *Jubilee, The Plough and the Stars, 4.48 Psychosis, Clowns/New Creation* and *Fatherland* (Lyric Hammersmith); *Julius Caesar* (Bridge Theatre); *Dirty Dancing: The Classic Story on Stage* (Phoenix Theatre); *Funny Girl* (Menier Chocolate Factory); *Sunny Afternoon* (Harold Pinter Theatre); *Sleeping Beauty* (Matthew Bourne's New Adventures) and *Wonderland* (Hampstead Theatre).

# THEATRE 503

Theatre503 is an award-winning theatre, which supports and stages more first-time writers than any other theatre in the country. At the heart of this commitment is a belief that the most important element in a writer's development is to see their work on a stage, in front of an audience, performed to the highest professional standard. Over 100 new pieces of work are staged at 503 in a year, ranging from 1-2 night short pieces to full length 4-week runs. Careers started at 503 include Tom Morton-Smith (*Oppenheimer*), Anna Jordan (*Yen*), Katori Hall (*The Mountaintop*), Jon Brittain (*Rotterdam*) – the last two productions started at 503 and won Olivier Awards.

## Theatre503 Team

| | |
|---|---|
| Artistic Director | Lisa Spirling |
| Executive Director | Andrew Shepherd |
| Producer | Jake Orr |
| Literary Manager | Steve Harper |
| Operations Manager | Anna De Freitas |
| Marketing Coordinator | Rebecca Usher |
| Technical Manager | Alastair Borland |
| Literary Associate | Lauretta Barrow |
| Resident Assistant Producers | Uju Enendu, Liam McLaughlin, Helen Milne, Jessica Moncur, Samara Thomas |
| Interns | Holly Dixon, Ean Wilson, Ane Miren Arriaga |

## Theatre503 Board

Erica Whyman (Chair)
Royce Bell (Vice Chair)
Chris Campbell
Joachim Fleury
Celine Gagnon
Eleanor Lloyd
Marcus Markou
Geraldine Sharpe-Newton
Jack Tilbury
Roy Williams OBE

## Theatre503 Volunteers

Emma Anderson, Emily Brearley-Bayliss, Ciaran Chillingworth, Debra Dempster, Abbie Duncanson, Claire Finn, Emma Griffiths, Tom Hartwell, Beatrice Hollands, Gareth Jones, George Linfield, Emrys Lloyd-Roberts, Ceri Lothian, Angelique MacDonald, Berit Moback, Olivia Munk, Christina Murdock, Denitsa Pashova, Annabel Pemberton, Evie Richards, Lucy Robson, Kate Roche, Sussan Sanii, Chloe Saunders, Laura Sedgwick, Paul Sockett, Aydan Tair, Sian Thomas, Stephanie Withers

# OUR SUPPORTERS

Theatre503's work would not be possible without the support of the following individuals, trusts and organisations:

We are particularly grateful to Philip and Christine Carne and the long-term support of The Carne Trust for our Playwriting Award and 503Five.

Our Current Patrons: Angela Hyde-Courtney, Cas & Philip Donald, Darryl Eales, David Baxter, Erica Whyman, Flow Associates, Geraldine Sharpe-Newton, Jill Segal, Kay Ellen Colsover, Marcus Markou, Michael North, Mike Morfey, Pam Alexander, Patricia Hamzahee and Rotha Bell

Arts Council England Grants for the Arts, The Boris Karloff Foundation, The Peter Wolff Trust, The Schroder Charity Trust, The Sylvia Waddilove Foundation, Unity Theatre Trust, Wandsworth Borough Council, The Golsoncott Foundation.

Nick Hern Books, The Harold Hyam Wingate Foundation, Curtis Brown and Ben Hall for their support of the Playwriting Award.

The Orseis Trust for their support of the 503Five

M&G Investments and Barbara Broccoli for their support of our Five-O-Fresh Young Creative Leaders Project.

Jack Tilbury, Plann, Dynamics, CharcoalBlue, Stage Solutions, Bush Theatre & Will Bowen for their support in refurbishing our seats.

Theatre503 is in receipt of funding from Arts Council England's Catalyst: Evolve fund, match funding every pound raised in new income until July 2019.

# THANKS

Theatre503 would like to thank the American Playwriting Foundation, Jerwood Space, Charlotte Bevan at the National Theatre, Graeae, Royal Exchange Theatre, Manchester, and Beth Blickers for their support on *Br'er Cotton*, Philip and Christine Carne for their generous donation for *Br'er Cotton*. Further thanks to Rosie Sheehy, Gwilym Lee, Malachi Kirby, Sarah Niles and Sidney Cole for the rehearsed reading of *Br'er Cotton*.

SUBSIDISED REHEARSAL FACILITIES PROVIDED BY

# JERWOOD SPACE

# BR'ER COTTON

Tearrance Arvelle Chisholm

## Characters

RUFFRINO / SON, *fourteen, male, black*
NADINE / MOTHER, *early thirties, female, black*
MATTHEW / GRANDFATHER, *sixties, male, black*
CAGED_BIRD99, *fourteen, female, white*
OFFICER, *mid-thirties, male, white*
REDNECK_SWAG, *disembodied white voice*

## Settings

The cotton field. Timeless.

The kitchen / cotton. A cotton field grows in a kitchen.
The kitchen is sinking.

Diaspora. A post-apocalyptic wasteland via Xbox.

## Time

Right-right now!

*This text went to press before the end of rehearsals and so may differ slightly from the play as performed.*

## ARS POETICA

*The cotton field.*

MOTHER, *a new mother, cradling an infant. Timeless.*

*This is a lullaby.* NADINE *fills the beats (...) with music.*

MOTHER. Once upon a time out of mind, this land was one great big tall hill.

...

The hill reached up forever; higher and higher. Past the clouds, past the stars, past the moon, to where if you stood on your tippiest-toe on the very top branch of the tallest tree on the highest peak with your arms stretched out as far as it could go, the tip of your longest finger would be just a hair length from touching heaven.

...

Livin' in the shadow of heaven made everybody terribly happy. Leastwise that's what they told themselves. Everybody spoke the same language and was generally on the same accord. And even when there were moments of difference, the difference was so slight that capitulation left no lasting wounds. And everyone was contented to live this way.

...

Everyone except Br'er Cotton.

...

...

Everyone on the hill used the same word for 'peculiar' and everyone agreed that Br'er Cotton was exactly that.

Because everyone grinned, and he scowled.

Because everyone whispered, and he screamed.

Because everyone sang,

...

and he cursed.

Because everyone was glad to live in such close proximity to heaven, but seeing heaven's gate from his front porch only served to taunt Br'er Cotton.

...

'Why should somethin' so good, be just out of my reach?', he fumed. 'Why can't I enjoy my heaven here on earth?'

...

The unfairness of it all infuriated Br'er Cotton to the point where he could only spit and grind his teeth. Till this one day, no special day in particular, save it was the day that he finally made his decision. On this very ordinary day Br'er Cotton decided he could take it no longer. He was gonna break into heaven.

...

...

...

**TWO BIRDS**

*Lynchburg, VA. The City of Seven Hills.*

*The eighth and forgotten, 'Cotton Hill'.*

*The hill is taking back the house.*

*A cotton field grows in a kitchen.*

*The kitchen is sinking.*

NADINE *enters. She's wearing a neon polo and khakis. The back of her shirt reads 'Lovely Maids'.*

*She uproots the table. And moves it to the other side of the room. She considers it. She uproots the chairs and moves them too. She considers all.*

MATTHEW *enters. He wears an ancient bathrobe. It looks as if it's made of tree bark. He has tufts of cotton in his hair. His eyes are tightly closed. He stumbles about blindly. He crashes into the newly placed table. He opens his eyes.*

MATTHEW. Damn it Nadine! Why is the table over here?

NADINE. I moved it.

MATTHEW....

(You moved it huh?)

*He considers this. He closes his eyes again and begins to make a mug of coffee.*

*He makes a great show of how difficult this is to do blind.* NADINE *ignores him.*

NADINE. I'm feng shui-ing.

MATTHEW. Feng shui-ing?

NADINE. Feng shui. It's the ancient Chinese art of furniture arrangin'.

MATTHEW. I know what it is.

NADINE....

MATTHEW. (Feng shui. Huh. Everythang we got is trash.)

…

Say, I wonder what this pile a trash look like in this corner? How 'bout we slide this heap uh junk 'gainst that wall. I thank a lil of that debris'll really open up the space. Huh!

*He knocks over his cup of coffee.*

Damn it!

*With his eyes still shut, he fumbles for a dish towel. He creates a bigger mess.*

NADINE. Goddammit you ol' fool! Move! You just spreading the mess around! You and your stupid ol'-man games.

What are you trying to prove stumblin' 'round with your eyes pent up anyhow?

NADINE *cleans up his mess.*

MATTHEW. I'm practicin'.

NADINE. Practicing for what?

MATTHEW. Not bein' able to see.

NADINE. You goin' blind now? You just come from the eye doctor and he ain't said nothin' 'bout you –

MATTHEW. Is he in my eyes? Can nat man see what I see? Ain't nothin' as clear or as bright as it usetuh be! Everythang dull! 'Cause…

NADINE. 'Cause what?

MATTHEW. 'Cause… I'm dyin', Nadine.

NADINE.…

Well… you mind hurryin' it along. I gotta get to work.

MATTHEW. Thas cold-blooded.

NADINE. I ain't got time to be foolin' with you today, Matthew.

MATTHEW. Ain't nobody foolin', Nay. Woke up this mornin' and there Death was, lyin' in the bed next to me. Got up and shaved and there he was starin' right back at me in the mirror. Grinnin'. Thas how come I'm pretendin' to be blind; I'm tired uh seein' his face. I figure, with the way he stalkin' me so, this likely be my last day on this here earth.

NADINE. Is that a fact?

MATTHEW. Sho. I think you oughta take the day off from work.

NADINE. Interestin'. That's the same mess you fed me yestaday. And like a fool I went ahead and stayed home – in spite of the fact you ain't name not a single tangible symptom. Then, soon as I call in, you miraculously got better. You even did ya calisthenics in the afternoon –

MATTHEW. Them calisthenics is the only thing that's keepin' this ol' ticker tickin'!

NADINE. I'm jus sayin'. I ain't seen no more signs of your impending bucket-kickin'. You was all better. Until now. Today. When I'm on my way out the do' again. If I didn't know no better, I'd say you didn't want me to work.

MATTHEW. Well –

NADINE. But that's crazy right? Seeing as how this family need all the money it can get.

MATTHEW. I got my retirement checks –

NADINE. Yeah, but you get your check on the first and by the fifth you askin' me to hold twenty dollars.

MATTHEW. Never you mind what I do with my check –

NADINE. Which is exactly why I gotta work.

MATTHEW. But do you gotta work for them?

NADINE. Who? Lovely Maids?

MATTHEW. No, not Lovely Maids –  But yes, Lovely Maids!

NADINE....

MATTHEW. Dontcha see?

NADINE....

MATTHEW. Do you gotta work for... white people?!

NADINE. I got all kinds of clients. I clean wherever they send me.

MATTHEW. That ain't the point, gal.

...

Yuh great-great-great-grandmother –

NADINE. Who was a slave.

MATTHEW. – cleaned some white man's house. Yuh great-great-grandmother cleaned some white man's house. Yuh great-grandmother cleaned some white man's house. Yuh grandmother, my mother, cleaned some white man's house. And yuh mother, God rest her soul, cleaned –

NADINE. Fine! I get it. I come from a long line of cleanin' women.

What of it?

MATTHEW. This family stuck in a rut, Nadine! And it ain't just the womenfolk neither. I worked at the cotton mill, my daddy worked at the cotton mill, my granddaddy picked cotton, my great-great –

NADINE. Fine, Matthew. I get it. We in a rut. What do you want me to do about it?

MATTHEW. Unrut us!

NADINE. And pray tell, just how am I supposed to do that?

MATTHEW. Quit.

NADINE. I cain't quit.

MATTHEW. Why not? You went to college.

NADINE. We done been over this time and time again. I went to Lynchburg College for one semester! I got a total of four, count 'em, four college credits.

MATTHEW. That's more than I got.

NADINE. Yeah, but it ain't enough.

MATTHEW. Enough for what?

NADINE. You think I want to clean up after folks for a living? Don't you think if I had any other choice I'd be doing something else?

MATTHEW. I think you think it's easier for you to settle, than it is to actually try.

NADINE. Now you wait a goddamn minute! You don't know shit 'bout what I'm tryin' to do! So just shut your damn mouth, ya hear!

MATTHEW. Jesus!

…

I wasn't trying to get nothin' started here, Nadine. I just thank each generation oughta do a lil better than the one that come befo' it. How come you think I went to all the trouble of settin' the bar so low?

RUFFRINO, *fourteen, enters. He's dressed in all black, with a black beret and dark shades. He looks rather militant. He has an overstuffed bookbag slung across his shoulder.*

Speak of the devil. It's Ruffrino. The last hope of the Witherspoon family legacy.

NADINE.…

MATTHEW.…

RUFFRINO. Wassup?

*The kitchen sinks a few inches.*

RUFFRINO *stumbles.*

Y'all feel that?

*They haven't.*

NADINE. Sit down, I'll make you some toast.

RUFFRINO. Naw, I'm good. I gotta get goin'.

NADINE. What's the rush? School don't start for another hour. You got plenty of time.

RUFFRINO. I'm going in early.

NADINE. For what?

RUFFRINO. No reason. I just gotta go.

NADINE. What are you up to?

RUFFRINO. Nothin'.

> NADINE *scrutinizes him.*

NADINE. You only wear that beret when you feelin' especially 'revolutionary'. What are you plannin'?

RUFFRINO. Nothin'. Damn.

NADINE. That's it. Open your bookbag.

RUFFRINO. What? Why?

NADINE. 'Cause the last time you was dressed like this you got suspended for inciting a riot.

RUFFRINO. It wasn't a riot, they just panicked because of the sirens. Some fuck shit –

MATTHEW. Watch that mouf!

NADINE. Either way, ya principal said anymore 'rebellious activities' and he was gonna let the police deal with you.

RUFFRINO. Fuck the po-lice!

MATTHEW. Watch that mouf!

RUFFRINO. Can I go now?

NADINE. Not until you open that bookbag.

RUFFRINO....

> Whatever.

> *He heaves the bookbag onto the table.*

NADINE. Open it.

RUFFRINO. You open it.

*An impasse.*

MATTHEW. I'll open it.

MATTHEW *opens the bookbag. He peers in hesitantly.*

It's paper. See Nay, nothing but papers and them ol' beat-up Black Panther books.

NADINE *inspects the bookbag, she pulls out the papers. She holds up a sheet, it has the face of a young black man on it.*

NADINE. Who is this?

RUFFRINO. D'Wayne Chambers.

NADINE. He a friend of yours?

RUFFRINO. A friend of mine? You can't be that oblivious! Hello! Wake up! Read a damn paper sometime –

MATTHEW. Ruffrino!

NADINE. Answer me now! Who is this? –

RUFFRINO. D'Wayne Chambers. The latest casualty in the war the white man is waging on young black men in this country. Shot and killed by the police for no other reason than he was young and black and thus a threat to the establishment. Ring any bells?

*In response,* NADINE *digs deeper into* RUFFRINO*'s bookbag.*

Don't look in that –

*She pulls out a bottle of lighter fluid.*

NADINE. Lighter fluid? What is this for?

RUFFRINO. An art project.

NADINE. You don't have art class.

*She digs further into the bag, a hidden compartment. She removes a small ax.*

Explain THIS, Ruffrino!

RUFFRINO. I don't have to explain myself to you –

NADINE *steps closer to* RUFFRINO. *A warning.*

NADINE. Answer me, or I swear 'fore God –

RUFFRINO *steps even closer to* NADINE.

RUFFRINO. What?

*They face off.*

MATTHEW. My daddy woulda laid me out where I stood if
I'da bucked at my momma the way you doin' –

RUFFRINO. Then do something about it, old man.

MATTHEW. Don't test me boy. I can still knock you clean into –

MATTHEW *lunges for* RUFFRINO, *but loses his footing
and stumbles.*

NADINE *is distracted.*

RUFFRINO *grabs his things and beelines for the door.*

*But* NADINE *is quick. She intercepts him.*

NADINE. Where you think you goin'?

RUFFRINO. Away!

NADINE. You ain't goin' nowhere until you tell me just what it
is you plannin' to do!

NADINE *grabs* RUFFRINO's *bookbag. They play tug o' war
over the bag for several beats. Until* RUFFRINO *lets go.*

NADINE *stumbles back and twists her ankle.*

*She fights back tears.*

MATTHEW. There! I hope you proud of yourself.

RUFFRINO. It wasn't my fault!

MATTHEW. And you used to be such a good kid, Ruffrino?
I don't know what's got into you. It's getting to where I cain't
stand you.

RUFFRINO. I can't stand you either!

NADINE. You ain't gonna be happy till them people done
thrown you out of that damn school!

RUFFRINO. Who cares. Nothing but zombies there anyway. The living dead.

NADINE. Well what you think the folks like in jail? 'Cause it's like you been throwing rocks at the prison lately. Thas where you wanna be? Jail?

RUFFRINO. You would love that wouldn't you? So you could pretend like I never happened just like my damn father –

NADINE *raises her hand to* RUFFRINO, *but she catches herself.*

NADINE. ENOUGH! ENOUGH! ENOUGH!

I am sick to death of the both of you.

MATTHEW. What I do?

*She cleans up* RUFFRINO's *mess.*

NADINE. It's like nobody else in this house is capable of thinkin' about anybody other than theyself! Between you and your 'deathbed'. And you concealin' weapons, tryin' to start the revolution, I ain't got nothing left! You two are runnin' me ragged. I'm in tatters! I'M FRAYED! FRAYED!

RUFFRINO. You so damn dramatic.

RUFFRINO *tries to leave, but* NADINE *stops him.*

NADINE. Oh no, no, no – You ain't goin' nowhere.

RUFFRINO. I gotta go to school don't I?

NADINE. I don't trust you, Ruffrino. And besides your grandfather is passin' on to the great by and by this afternoon, so here's what's gonna happen: Ruffrino you stayin' at home and lookin' after your grandfather. And Matthew you be in charge of keepin' this boy from self-destruction. Two birds!

MATTHEW. Nadine!                    RUFFRINO. Nadine!

*The kitchen sinks a few more inches.*

RUFFRINO *is the only one that notices.*

**NADINE CLEANS**

*Another room in another home. Or at least the suggestion of one.*

NADINE *cleans her life away.*

NADINE....

    NADINE *cleans.*

    ...

    NADINE *cleans.*

    ...

    NADINE *cleans.*

    ...

    NADINE *cleans.*

    ...

    NADINE *cleans.*

    ...

    NADINE *cleans.*

    ...

    NADINE *cleans.*

    ...

    NADINE *cleans.*

    ...

    NADINE *cleans.*

    ...

    NADINE *cleans.*

    ...

    NADINE *cleans.*

**EVERYTHING**

*The kitchen / cotton field.*

*A cart with a TV and an Xbox has been rolled into the room.*

MATTHEW *and* RUFFRINO *sit at the kitchen table.*
MATTHEW *is lost in a story;* RUFFRINO *is lost in the TV.*

MATTHEW....So once he decided that he was gonna break into heaven he ate a spoonful of clabber, tucked in his socks, and set out on his journey...

MATTHEW *realizes* RUFFRINO *isn't paying attention.*

Hello? Earth to Ruffrino!

RUFFRINO....

MATTHEW. HELLO!

RUFFRINO. What? Oh. Good story, Matthew.

MATTHEW. You wasn't even payin' attention.

RUFFRINO....

MATTHEW. Dadgummit! Hello!

RUFFRINO. What!?

MATTHEW. You aint lis'nin' to me!

RUFFRINO. I'm busy.

MATTHEW. Busy wit what?

(What is this world coming to when a ol' man cain't run off at the mouth and have somebody lissen at him?)

RUFFRINO *stares at the TV.*

Will you turn that idiot box off? I'm testifyin' over here!

RUFFRINO. Matthew! Shhhhhhh!

MATTHEW. And thas another thing, how come you callin' me Matthew?

RUFFRINO....

MATTHEW. HELLO!

RUFFRINO. What?

MATTHEW. How come you call me Matthew.

RUFFRINO. Because. It's your name.

MATTHEW. I know that! But it used to be in my day merely living longa than anotha person entitled you to a few inalienable privileges. One of which was the addressment by certain basic titles from they youngers.

RUFFRINO. Such as?

MATTHEW. Y'know… sir. Ma'am. Mister. Miss. Momma. Daddy. Granddaddy –

RUFFRINO. I am not callin' you 'Granddaddy'.

MATTHEW. Why not?

RUFFRINO. It sound gay.

MATTHEW.…

RUFFRINO. 'Grandaddy'.

MATTHEW. Well, if you say it like that.

RUFFRINO *returns to staring at the TV.*

*Suddenly:*

RUFFRINO. Damn it! Nadine fucked everything up! I can't believe she took my shit!

MATTHEW. Hush all that cussin' –

RUFFRINO. Look at what's going on. Today was the day. I tweeted to all my followers that today was the day for my… art project. Now I'ma look like some whack loser. 'Sorry guys, can't start the revolution today, my mommy won't let me out to play.'

MATTHEW. Revolution? Huh.

RUFFRINO. Don't worry about it. It'll be televised.

MATTHEW. Huh. Jus' what was you plannin' to do anyhow?

RUFFRINO. Wake up the fuckin' zombies.

MATTHEW. I ain't gon tell you again about that mouf! Show me some respect.

RUFFRINO. Whatever.

MATTHEW. Now, how you supposed to wake up these 'zombies' as you say?

With some lighter fluid and a hatchet? Whas a few pictures of some dead boy supposed to do? Answer me that.

RUFFRINO. Make them think! Open their eyes. Show them: Black lives matter! Black kids, that look just like me, are getting shot down. Left and right! And nobody cares! Nobody sees!

MATTHEW. Some folks is gon' see what they see, regardless of what they see.

RUFFRINO. Still –

MATTHEW. Black lives matter? Huh. You a hypocrite, you know that right?

RUFFRINO. What are you talkin' about?

MATTHEW. You talk the talk, but you ain't walkin' the walk. You s'posed to be Mr Pro-Black, Ruffrino X and such, but you don't show a lickuh respect for the 'black lives' thas livin' right up under the same roof as you.

RUFFRINO....

MATTHEW. Ain't got nothin' to say that, huh?

RUFFRINO. You know what? You right.

MATTHEW. I'm right? Huh. Well, knock me over with a feather!

RUFFRINO. Don't act so surprised. I hear the truth when it's put to me. You right. The revolution starts at home. We ain't never gonna be able to rise up against the oppressive regime of the white man if we fighting in our homes. That's exactly what they want us to do.

MATTHEW. It sounds like you sayin' you owe me an apology.

RUFFRINO....

I'll call you 'Pops'. Occasionally. That's the best I can do.

MATTHEW *beams*.

MATTHEW. You owe yo mama an apology at least.

RUFFRINO. I didn't mean what I said, she just make me so mad.

MATTHEW. Her and everybody else these days. You just angry in general.

RUFFRINO. I am.

MATTHEW. Well whatchu got to be so angry about?

RUFFRINO. Everything!

MATTHEW. Everything like what?

RUFFRINO. Everything!

MATTHEW. Well, name me jus' one thing. For an example. A for instance…

RUFFRINO. For instance, right now, I'm pissed off at you!

MATTHEW. Good. And now, why you mad at me for?

RUFFRINO. I'm mad I gotta explain it! I'm mad you don't just get it!

I'm mad you ain't pissed off too!

MATTHEW. What I got to be mad about?

RUFFRINO. EVERYTHING!

MATTHEW. You talk in circles.

…

Teenage angst. That's all that is. You'll grow out of it.

RUFFRINO. (Unless I get shot and killed first.)

RUFFRINO *returns to staring at the TV.*

MATTHEW. Don't get too comfortable in front of that television, my stories come on in an hour and I gotta see if Juliana comes out of her coma... What's that you watchin' anyhow?

RUFFRINO. MSNBC.

MATTHEW. Is that lady that look like a man on nere? I like it when that lady that look like a man be on nere –

RUFFRINO. Shhhhhhh!

MATTHEW. Shush me again here –

RUFFRINO. This is live coverage. They waiting to hear the results of the Grand Jury. They decidin' wether or not that racist pig bastard that murdered D'Wayne Chambers is gonna be brought up on charges.

MATTHEW. Now where was this? Up in Cleveland?

RUFFRINO. No. That was last week. No Charges.

MATTHEW. Oh. This down in Texas?

RUFFRINO. No that was the week before last. No charges.

MATTHEW. This the one in Baltimore den?

RUFFRINO. Nope. That was last month. No charges.

MATTHEW. New York?

RUFFRINO. No charges.

MATTHEW. St. Louis?

RUFFRINO. No charges.

MATTHEW. Minnesota.

RUFFRINO. No. Charges.

MATTHEW....

RUFFRINO. This happened in Charlottesville.

MATTHEW. Charlottesville? That's just up the highway a spell –

RUFFRINO. Right.

MATTHEW. It's getting closer then.

RUFFRINO. Right.

MATTHEW *and* RUFFRINO *stare at the television.*

MATTHEW. So they just shot this boy?

RUFFRINO. In the street like a dog. Actually dogs get more respect.

MATTHEW. What was he doing?

RUFFRINO. What do you mean?

MATTHEW. To get himself shot. He must've been doing something.

RUFFRINO. It doesn't matter what he was doing, he doesn't deserve to be shot and killed like that.

MATTHEW. But he was doin' something? Right?

RUFFRINO. He resisted arrest – allegedly –

MATTHEW. See. There.

RUFFRINO. 'See. There.' What? That doesn't mean he should be killed.

If he was white they wouldn't've –

MATTHEW. But see he's not white. That's the problem with negroes these days. They want rules that don't apply to them, to apply to them.

RUFFRINO. But there should be one set of rules for everybody.

MATTHEW. But that ain't the case. And I ain't sayin' it's fair. But it ain't about bein' fair or unfair, it's about the way things are being the way things are. You gotta accept your circumstances.

See now I wish I could eat collard greens and hog maws, but the doctor said sautéed kale and turkey bacon is better for me. So what I eat? Kale and turkey bacon with a lil EVOO. And that ain't fair, 'cause turkey bacon is a lie. But I do it, 'cause them's my rules and if I wanna keep livin' I'ma follow 'em. The problem is negroes these days don't know the rules.

RUFFRINO. We ain't talking about turkey bacon. We talkin'
about life. We talkin' about being treated as equals. We're
talkin' about not being shot down in the streets and the pigs
gettin' off scott free. There should be –

MATTHEW *lies down on the floor.*

MATTHEW. There's that word again. 'Should'. I ain't concerned
with 'should'. I'm concerned with 'is'. Things 'is' the way
they 'is'. And maybe things could change, but they haven't in
my lifetime, which leads me to believe that they ain't gonna.
Now grab my ankles. It's time for my calisthenics?

RUFFRINO *holds* MATTHEW'*s ankles in the sit-up position.*

You know what your real problem is, Ruff. You too serious.
You like your father.

RUFFRINO. If I had a nickel.

MATTHEW. Your father was a good man – Is a good man. He
ain't dead.

RUFFRINO. Fifty-years-to-life good?

MATTHEW. Okay. He a man. Maybe a little less emphasis on
the good part. He took care of you and your mother. Until
he didn't.

RUFFRINO. Just another black man who fell victim to the
systematic separation of the black family perpetuated by the
white man since slavery. The black family must be vigilant –

MATTHEW. I don't know about all that…

MATTHEW *does sit-ups.*

But one day you'll become a man. Wit full rights and
privileges. You'll encounter many another man on the road.
When you do. You stand up straight. Look him square in the
eyes. And shake his hand. Firm grip. And you can count
yourself. Just as good as any other man. But one day. You'll
come across anotha fella. And he gonna be your better. In
every conceivable way. And you won't have to bow down
formally. It's more carnal than that. His man-scent'll top your

man-scent. And you'll realize. The only reason. You've been in charge. Up to that point. Is because he hadn't been around.

RUFFRINO. You sound like a slave.

MATTHEW. That man for me. Was your father. It's a peculiar thing to have the man that comes for your daughter to be your better. But then I left the do' wide open for folks to be better than me...

RUFFRINO. What are you even talkin' about?

MATTHEW. An old man oughta be able to sit and run off at the mouf and have some body lissen at him – No. Not just lissen at him, but really pay attention. Pay close attention to him; and his words. 'Cause if you lissen and pay close enough attention, he might just let slip where he been hiding his treasures.

RUFFRINO. Treasures? What are you some kinda pirate or something?

MATTHEW. Wouldn't you like to know.

RUFFRINO....

MATTHEW....

RUFFRINO. You ain't holding out on us? Is you? Pops?

MATTHEW. Pops? Huh. I like that –

RUFFRINO. Is you?

MATTHEW. So now, all of sudden, you tryin' to hear what I got to say. Now that the subject of money come up.

RUFFRINO. Money? Who said anything about money? Are you hiding money?

MATTHEW. Maybe I is. Maybe I ain't.

RUFFRINO. OH MY GOD! That's why you don't ever have any money. That's why we don't ever see your check –

MATTHEW. Never you mind what I do with my check.

RUFFRINO. Are you kidding me! You got Nadine cleanin' toilets to keep the lights on, all the while you sittin' on stacks.

MATTHEW. Forget it. I shouldn't've brought it up.

RUFFRINO. It take an old negro like you to sit around and hoard dollars. It's not your fault, it's a systematic distrust in financial institutions bred into us to keep us disenfranchised. But still... Where is it? How much you got stashed away –

MATTHEW. Ain't no secret stash. I was just talkin' out the side of my neck. Just provin' a point.

RUFFRINO. Which is?

MATTHEW. That you oughta listen to an old man when he talkin'. 'Cause an old man is like a box of chocolate: You never know what you gonna get.

RUFFRINO. I'm tellin' Nadine.

MATTHEW. Don't say nothin' to Nadine! Ain't no money. Ain't no stash. Ain't no treasure. So just keep your mouth shut!

RUFFRINO. Let me find out...

## NADINE STUDIES

*Another room in another home. Or at least the suggestion of one.*

NADINE *sits at a table with several books.*

NADINE....

　NADINE *studies.*

　...

　NADINE *studies.*

　...

　NADINE *studies.*

　*Suddenly* OFFICER *enters. He's dressed in full police uniform. The chatter from his radio can be heard intermittently.*

　*He watches* NADINE.

　*At length* NADINE *notices him. She panics! She stands and throws her hands up in the air.*

　My hands are up! Don't shoot!

OFFICER. What are –

NADINE. Lovely Maids! I work here. They pay for three hours but they keep the house so clean it only takes me fifteen minutes. Then I do my homework. I know it's wrong. It's stealing. Technically. But I ain't think it was no reason to call the police on me. Oh Lord –

OFFICER. Calm down –

NADINE. Calm down he says. I can't calm down. I can't be arrested. I ain't got the time to be arrested –  I ain't got the money to get arrested –

OFFICER. Relax. I'm not the police.

NADINE. You sure look like one.

OFFICER. I mean. I am. A cop. But I'm not here for you. This is my house.

NADINE. Oh. I don't mean to gyp you. It's just it's my only time to study. When I'm not at school, I'm at work, and when I'm not at either one of them, I'm at home. And I can't do my homework at home. I shoulda told somebody y'all was overpaying, but I thought they might give me another house and then I'd lose this time. And I'd flunk out of college. Again. And I also sorta liked the idea of getting paid to do my homework – but that's got nothing to do with you. What do you care about my woes? I'll just be going now and I'll have Lovely Maids adjust the schedule. I'm so sorry. Again.

*She packs her things.*

OFFICER. Don't leave on my account.

NADINE....

OFFICER. Why don't you just sit back down, and finish your homework.

NADINE. Now what now?

OFFICER. I mean you been doing it all this time and it hasn't bothered me. So why should it start bothering me now? 'Cause I know?

NADINE. Thas a good point.

OFFICER. Besides, I wouldn't want to be the reason you flunked out of college. Again. So. Please. Stay.

NADINE. I do have a lot of reading to do... Are you sure you don't mind?

OFFICER. As long as you don't mind if I make myself a sandwich.

NADINE. Just don't make a mess, I just finished wiping – This is your house. By all means.

OFFICER. Thanks.

NADINE *sits back down at the table.*

*Tentatively.*

OFFICER *makes a sandwich.*

NADINE *studies.*

NADINE....

OFFICER *makes a sandwich.*

OFFICER....

NADINE *studies.*

NADINE....

OFFICER *makes a sandwich.*

*Suddenly.*

| | |
|---|---|
| NADINE. This is weird. | OFFICER. What're you studying? |
| What? | What? |
| Oh. Biology. | What's weird? |
| What? | What? |

NADINE. This is strange. I'm just gonna go.

*She packs her things again.*

OFFICER. Really. Stay. I'm paying, remember? And...

*He shakes crumbs onto the counter.*

You missed a spot.

NADINE....

OFFICER. Seriously. I don't mind the company.

NADINE. Okay...

*She sits back down. She picks up a book.*

OFFICER. Biology, huh?

NADINE. 101. I'm studying nursing at Lynchburg College. I want to be a neonatal nurse.

OFFICER. Premature babies right?

NADINE. Yeah. I heard somewhere that preemies don't cry. Something about that appeals to me.

OFFICER. Hmm.

NADINE. That's the first time I've said that out loud.

OFFICER. Said what out loud?

NADINE. That I want to be a neonatal nurse. That I want to be anything really.

OFFICER. How come?

NADINE. I don't know. Saying it out loud makes it real. And that makes me… nervous.

OFFICER. I bet you'll make a great nurse.

NADINE. You don't know anything about me.

OFFICER. Sure I do. You're clean. Dirt isn't good for babies. And you're good at multitasking. And you're honest… when you get caught at least!

NADINE. I knew it! You just stallin' till the boys in blue get here.

OFFICER. I'm kidding.

NADINE. So was I.

OFFICER.…

NADINE. I really am honest though.

OFFICER. Okay. Then what made you tell me you wanted to be a nurse, just now? Honestly.

NADINE. I guess it's 'cause I don't know you. If I told the people that knew me, they would laugh in my face.

OFFICER. Why?

NADINE. Because. I ain't particularly suited to be no nurse. I ain't got no bedside manner to speak of. I'm the worst in a stressful situation. And I can't stand the sight of blood, or people in pain, or needles –

OFFICER. So then why take up nursing?

NADINE. This is starting to feel like an interrogation.

OFFICER. This is a conversation. An actual conversation. Don't ruin it.

NADINE. I don't know. Nursing is a time-honored profession. It's notable. It's a job you can be proud of.

OFFICER. But you can admit that you're not suited for it.

NADINE. It'll come. If I stick with it and keep studying and practicing, what I need will come.

OFFICER *laughs, but not at her.*

What's so funny?

OFFICER. Hope. It's female trait.

NADINE....

OFFICER. Only a woman can honestly believe that a person can change. That was my wife's favorite thing to say to me. 'Don't worry. It'll come.'

NADINE. And did it?

OFFICER. It never came. And she went.

NADINE. Oh.

NADINE *studies.*

OFFICER *eats.*

What didn't come?

OFFICER *eats.*

Never mind –

OFFICER *eats.*

OFFICER. You know it was my wife's idea for me to become a cop. She told me to go down to the Emerson Building on Tuesday at 3 p.m. She said it didn't have to be that Tuesday, any Tuesday would do. So I let a few weeks pass because... I'm a man.

NADINE. Mmm-hmmm.

OFFICER. And then I went on down there. Turns out it was the recruitment office of the Lynchburg PD. My wife had heard that Lynchburg was so hard up for cops that they were taking anybody who showed up and could walk and chew gum at the same time. And seeing that I fit the bill, I walked right in, 'cause there wasn't a line, I signed my name, and was sworn in as the newest inductee of the Lynchburg Police Academy right there on the spot.

NADINE. That easy huh?

OFFICER. Pretty much.

NADINE. Well what I'm foolin' wit school for? I oughta just be a cop, right?

OFFICER. You could. They take anybody.

NADINE. Well thanks...

OFFICER. I didn't mean it like that. I'm just saying you could easily become a cop and you don't have to go to school for four years.

NADINE. It's fine. I ain't trying to be no cop. My son would kill me.

OFFICER. Look. I don't want you to think that I'm low-grading the LPD. There are some really great men on the force and they risk everything. Every day. But sometimes I wonder if being a cop was in more of a demand these days would some of us have made the cut. Hell, I probably wouldn't have.

NADINE. What makes you say that?

OFFICER. I'm not exactly suited for it.

NADINE. You look like the type.

OFFICER. Yeah but, I'm non-confrontational. A pacifist really. I don't like to raise my voice if I don't have to. Guns give me the willies, and I don't like donuts.

NADINE. So then why become a cop?

OFFICER. Because. It's a... how'd you put it? 'A time-honored profession.' Cops are symbols of courage and valor, like modern-day knights.

NADINE. And you ain't that?

OFFICER. But I stuck with it, because like you, my wife hoped that I could change. 'Don't worry, it'll come.' She said. And so I went to the academy every day, and every day I wondered: Is this the day they'll teach me to be brave? To be noble? Is this the day that I'll learn to be a hero? But that day never came. In fact, they weren't even expecting that of me. Being a cop is just mitigating risk so that you make it home at the end of your shift.

NADINE. Story of my life.

OFFICER. My wife used to remind me. Every day. 'Come home safe.' Every day. Like if she didn't say it, I would forget and get myself killed. Every day. Like it wasn't the one thought I had racing through my head from the moment I punched in.

NADINE. And so how is that? Being a thing you know you not suited for?

OFFICER. It's exhausting.

NADINE. Oh.

OFFICER. You want my advice?

NADINE. Sure.

OFFICER. Pick another career, quick, before you're seven years in and stuck.

NADINE. Matthew – my dad, was so proud of me the first time I was in college. I know it broke his heart when I flunked out after one semester.

OFFICER. Partied too hard?

NADINE. Pregnant.

OFFICER. Same thing I guess.

NADINE. Don't get me wrong. I love my son. He's the best thing I've done so far.

OFFICER. Of course.

NADINE. I just want my daddy to be proud of me again. So, I'm sticking with it this time. I'm doing it for him.

OFFICER. And I did it for my wife. I'm telling you, it's not enough.

NADINE. Maybe not for you but –

OFFICER. If you could be anything in the world, no limitations or expectations, what would you wanna be when you grew up?

NADINE. You wanna know the awful secret? I like being a cleaning lady. It bothers other people more than it bothers me.

OFFICER. Really?

NADINE. Yeah. I mean a clean toilet is a beautiful thing. It's quantifiable. It's a task with a definitive ending. And once it's done you can look at it and say that it's complete. An achievement. And it makes me feel good about myself. And even though they don't give degrees out for it, it's still got to be worth something.

OFFICER. Sure but –

NADINE. But what?

OFFICER. You mean to tell me that if you could be anything, anything in the entire world, you would choose to clean toilets?

NADINE. Sure?

OFFICER....

NADINE. I've never said that out loud either. That's pathetic ain't it?

OFFICER. Yeah. It is. But it's okay. I'm pathetic too.

NADINE *considers this. She realizes she's been insulted.*

NADINE. I ain't pathetic! And now, you can go on and be pathetic if you want to, but just leave me the hell out of it!

OFFICER. I just –

NADINE. Just because you never cut it as a cop doesn't mean I can't become a nurse. Nursing and policing is two different things. We are two different people. Entirely! And I ain't ask for your advice, or your opinion –

OFFICER. Actually you asked for both.

NADINE *packs her things*.

NADINE. Well that was my bad. And staying here was a mistake. I won't study here no more, the feng shui is all fucked up anyhow!

NADINE *storms out*.

NADINE *storms back in*.

I'm gonna be a nurse, damn it! I'm gonna be a neonatal fuckin' nurse, and I'm gonna nurse the hell out of little babies that don't cry. And I'm gonna be damn good at it too. I'll become the person I need to be, and I ain't gonna wind up sad and alone and pathetic like you! And you can put that in the bank!

NADINE *storms out again*.

OFFICER....

OFFICER *considers all*.

## DIASPORA

*A post-apocalyptic wasteland, or at least the suggestion of one.*

RUFFRINO *is garbed in post-apocalyptic armor; a pastiche of everyday found objects. He wields a righteous futuristic rifle.*

CAGED_BIRD99, *of a similar age, she's dressed similarly, save for a lucha mask that obscures her face. She's outfitted with a bazooka.*

*They fend off the zaliens (zombie aliens).*

CAGED_BIRD99. Cover me!

RUFFRINO. I got your back, Cagedbird.

*He zaps a zalien.*

CAGED_BIRD99. Thanks, RuffandRino. I can always count on you!

*They fend off the zaliens.*

RUFFRINO. Zalien scout three o'clock. Decapitate him before he has a chance to alert the zalien infantry –

CAGED_BIRD99. Too late! Check your radar. There's a level-seven zalien army headed our way. They've got a tank! Retreat! Retreat! –

RUFFRINO. No! Let's stand our ground. I'm trying to unlock the Tantalite Broadsword. I need the XP.

CAGED_BIRD99. In that case… IT'S. ABOUT. TO GO. DOWN.

*They brace for the onslaught of zalien soldiers –*

*Suddenly: the whisper of a sniper's bullet.*

RUFFRINO *collapses to the ground silently.*

*PROJECTION: 'RUFFandRINO has been sniped by redneck_swag'.*

*A second bullet.*

CAGED_BIRD99 *is also hit. She slumps over.*

*PROJECTION: 'CAGED_BIRD99 has been owned by redneck_swag'.*

*They lie on the ground. Dead.*

...

RUFFRINO *respawns.*

RUFFRINO. Fuck you redneck_swag!

REDNECK_SWAG (*a disembodied teenage boy's voice*). Fuck you. I'm the master! Bow down to your master! BOW DOWN!

CAGED_BIRD99 *respawns.*

CAGED_BIRD99. Sniping is for noobs. It's cheap.

REDNECK_SWAG. WANH! WANH! WANH! FUCKYOU!

RUFFRINO. NO, FUCKYOU –

CAGED_BIRD99. Ignore him. He's just trolling us.

RUFFRINO. I bet your mom and dad are cousins, you inbred fuck –

REDNECK_SWAG. FUCK YOU. NIGGER!! YOU FUCKING NIGGERS. EAT SHIT AND DIE. NIGGERS!! NIGGER! FUCKING NIGGER!

RUFFRINO. You white-trash piece of shit –

REDNECK_SWAG. FUCKYOU!! DIE NIGGER. DIEEEE! DIIIIIIIEEEEEEE!!! –

*PROJECTION: 'redneck_swag has logged off'.*

RUFFRINO. FUUUUCCCKKK!!

CAGED_BIRD99. Br'er. My ears.

RUFFRINO. Sorry. That shit really pisses me off – I FUCKIN' HATE WHITE PEOPLE!

CAGED_BIRD99. What are you supposed to do when the rage overwhelms you?

RUFFRINO. Count ten!

CAGED_BIRD99. So…

RUFFRINO. One, two, three, four –

CAGED_BIRD99. Slowly. Breathe.

RUFFRINO. Five… six… seven… eight… nine… ten.

CAGED_BIRD99. Better?

RUFFRINO. Yeah.

CAGED_BIRD99. Within you is a seed of great change, but you can't let anger blind you. Remember: Anger is a stone cast into a wasp's nest.

RUFFRINO. Deep.

   …

   Thanks.

CAGED_BIRD99. For what?

RUFFRINO. For always being the Martin to my Malcolm.

CAGED_BIRD99. Did you just compare me to Dr King? Honored, br'er.

RUFFRINO. I mean it. I don't fit in with the zombies at school. I don't fit with the zombies at home. It's like, where do I belong? Ya know?

CAGED_BIRD99. I know exactly how you feel.

RUFFRINO. Of course you do. You not 'sleep like everybody else. Before I heard you broadcasting your poetry over Xbox Live I thought I was the only conscious black kid in the whole world. I know you supposed to be all 'Kumbaya' and shit, but there's rage in your poetry. It spoke to me. We're like… soulmates.

*Awkward.*

CAGED_BIRD99. Speaking of which… I've been working on a new piece.

RUFFRINO. Lay it on me.

CAGED_BIRD99. It's called 'Language of the Outnumbered'.

RUFFRINO. I like it already.

CAGED_BIRD99. It's fresh so, bear with me.

(*Slam poetry.*)

We meet over time and space
Yet our words are the same
Despite our difference, we're the same
Because I'm broken and you broke
We use the same words to break
We use the same words to cry
The same words to hurt
We speak the same language, you and I
The language of the outnumbered.

*Suddenly,* MATTHEW *enters in his bathrobe.*

MATTHEW. What the – What is this?

RUFFRINO. I'm playing *Diaspora*.

CAGED_BIRD99. Who's that?

RUFFRINO. Matthew. The old man that lives in our house.

CAGED_BIRD99. Oh. I got one of those too.

MATTHEW. Well pause this mess. My stories is on and I told
you not to let me nap too long.

RUFFRINO. I can't pause it. It's live.

MATTHEW. What's live?

RUFFRINO. *Diaspora*. I'm online.

MATTHEW. Well I'ma online yo' butt if you don't turn this
mess off. I'm missin' my stories.

RUFFRINO. Yo, Cagedbird –

CAGED_BIRD99. I get it. You gotta go. My thumbs hurt

anyway. I need food. Later, br'er.

RUFFRINO. Later days.

RUFFRINO *and* MATTHEW *exit*.

*PROJECTION: 'RUFFandRINO has logged off'.*

CAGED_BIRD99 *is alone in the space. She removes her mask, to reveal that she's a teenage white girl.*

*She takes up a hidden pair of forearm crutches, revealing that she is physically disabled.*

*She exits.*

*PROJECTION: 'CAGED_BIRD99 has logged off'.*

## THE WITHERSPOON FAMILY CURSE

*The kitchen / cotton field.*

MATTHEW *and* RUFFRINO *in the kitchen.*

*They sit in front of the TV.* MATTHEW *wields the Xbox controller.*

RUFFRINO. Don't just stand there. Shoot!

MATTHEW. Somebody's a-comin'.

RUFFRINO. I know. Shoot him!

MATTHEW. Why I wanna go an' do that for?

RUFFRINO. Pops! That's a zalien footsoldier. Half-zombie, half-alien, hell-bent on the destruction of mankind!

MATTHEW. Well, heck, I betta shoot him then.

RUFFRINO. He's biting you!

MATTHEW. Well how do I shoot?

RUFFRINO. Press the 'A' button.

MATTHEW. Now which one is that now?

RUFFRINO. Green! Green! Green!

MATTHEW. Oh. I can't see – hand me my glasses.

RUFFRINO. It's too late! The zalien swarm has overrun your position. They're eating your brains.

MATTHEW. Oh my. That is gruesome. That is… what is that?

RUFFRINO. It's his spleeeen!

MATTHEW. And this don't turn your stomach none?

RUFFRINO. This is nothing. When the zalien queen bites you, your stomach explodes and your last meal splatters on the screen. Nachos!

MATTHEW *stares at* RUFFRINO. *He smiles.*

Why are you making that dopey face?

MATTHEW. Nothin'. You just acting like your old self just now. Before you got so deep off in them books your daddy sent you.

RUFFRINO. Before I woke up you mean?

MATTHEW. If that's whachu wanna call it – before you started mouthin' off, and gettin' into trouble at school – Now, explain to me again, what was you plannin' to do today?

RUFFRINO. I was gonna wake them up.

MATTHEW. Who?

RUFFRINO. The zombies.

MATTHEW. With lighter fluid and a hatchet.

RUFFRINO. Yes.

MATTHEW. You was gonna wake them up?

RUFFRINO. Yes.

MATTHEW. 'Cause they asleep?

RUFFRINO. Comatose.

MATTHEW. Okay, so let's say… best-case scenario you wake them up. Then what?

RUFFRINO. Then they'll see.

MATTHEW. See what exactly?

RUFFRINO. The truth.

MATTHEW. 'Cause they awake? They got they eyes open? They can see the truth?

RUFFRINO. Right.

MATTHEW. Okay. Then what?

RUFFRINO. Then what, what?

MATTHEW. Then what happens, all the people is woke and they eyes is open. And they walkin' round seein' the truth and thangs. Then what happen?

RUFFRINO. Then we change things.

MATTHEW. Change? Is that what you after? You trying to change things?

RUFFRINO. Yes. I'm trying to change the world –

MATTHEW *laughs*.

*And laughs*.

*And laughs*.

*And cries and laughs*.

I guess I missed the joke.

MATTHEW. This being my last day on earth, thas probably gon' be my last good laugh. I thank you for it.

RUFFRINO. What's so funny?

MATTHEW. You. You doin' all this for change! That's rich.

RUFFRINO....

MATTHEW. Boy, don't you know you ain't capable of changing nothing but your underwear. You gon' change the world? Huh.

RUFFRINO. Why not me? I gotta chance. I got more of a chance than you. Because I'm doing something. I'm trying. You don't do nothing.

MATTHEW. I beg your pardon. Doing nothin' is an art and I've mastered it. Second off, I ain't got no aims at changin' the world. 'Cause I know what I am.

RUFFRINO. Asleep.

MATTHEW. No. I'm a Witherspoon. Of the Amherst County Witherspoons.

RUFFRINO. Meaning?

MATTHEW. Meaning, the Witherspoons ain't no revolutionary figures. We ain't the changers. We the carry-on-ers. We the gettin'-by-ers.

RUFFRINO. You a crazy old fool. You know that Matthew?

MATTHEW. Witherspoons ain't remarkable. We don't do no revolutionizing. If and when it's time for that, we leave that work to better men than us. We become the minions. The pawns. We wind up casualties. The ones that make up the big numbers. They may etch our tiny Witherspoon name on giant monuments. One tiny name out of millions of other tiny names, but they ain't building no statues of no Witherspoons. 'Cause we the stay-out-of-it-ers. You come from a long line of that-ain't-got-nothing-to-do-with-me-ers.

RUFFRINO. So you mean to tell me, that no other Witherspoon? Ever? Anywhere? Did anything revolutionary? None of us have done anything of any importance? Ever?

MATTHEW. That is correct.

RUFFRINO. ...

MATTHEW. The last Witherspoon who tried was your great-great-great-great-great-grand-uncle Ingraham Witherspoon. Back in 1865 –

RUFFRINO. 1865!

MATTHEW. Your grand-uncle Ingraham was a slave. He lived on a cotton plantation. Right here in Amherst County. It was just down 29 a-ways, back behind where the old Food Lion used to be. It's towards the end of the war. Confederates was losin'. Losin' bad. They desperate. They decree that slaves could enlist. 'General Order Numba Fourteen'. Say it's for a new black infantry startin' up down in Richmond. Say if they fight for honor and country – two things that ain't never served no Witherspoon, mind you... If they fight true they can earn they freedom. They'll be paid a wage. And given a brand-new uniform with a pair of fine leather boots. Now, your grand-uncle Ingraham wasn't no fool. Every generation or so we get us a brilliant one. He was a brilliant one. I think you might be one too. I thought your mother was one but she... Anyhow. He was like you. Could see things for what they were and was pissed off about it. He knew better than to believe them white folk, 'specially when they was desperate.

But he had a plan. He was gon' 'change' things. So he signed on the dotted line, with an 'X', 'cause he couldn't write. And he went off with that man to Richmond. And now while they was trainin' and drillin' during the day, nights he was creepin' round in the shadows, whispering in negroes' ears. Sayin' things like 'Why should we fight for honor and country? We oughta fight for ourselves.' And before long he had him a coup in the works.

RUFFRINO. Dope. So then what happened?

MATTHEW. He died by firing squad.

RUFFRINO. What – How?

MATTHEW. The Witherspoon family curse is how. Whispered the right thing to the wrong person. Some other pawn ratted him out. But them Confederates kept they word. They set him free. So to speak. And they sent his uniform to his momma.

RUFFRINO. Is this another one of your old-man-treasure tales.

MATTHEW. It's true. I got his uniform to prove it.

RUFFRINO. You have grand-uncle Ingraham's uniform. You have a Confederate uniform. From 1865?

MATTHEW. Everything 'cept the boots.

RUFFRINO. Where? I've never seen it.

MATTHEW. I ain't never showed it to you.

RUFFRINO. Where is it then?

MATTHEW. It's safe. Bought one of them Space Bags. Sucked it flat with your momma's vacuum. They waterproof ya know?

RUFFRINO. The uniform?

MATTHEW. The Space Bags!

RUFFRINO. And you've got it stashed somewhere in this house?

MATTHEW. It's around.

RUFFRINO....

MATTHEW....

RUFFRINO. What else you got hid around here?

MATTHEW. Wouldn't you like to know.

RUFFRINO....

MATTHEW....

RUFFRINO. Where's the money, Matthew?

MATTHEW. Oh, it's in the – Ha. Ha. You ain't slick. There ain't no money!

MATTHEW *exits*.

RUFFRINO *considers all*.

*The kitchen sinks a few more inches*.

RUFFRINO *discovers a cotton boll peeking through the linoleum*.

**I FEEL LIKE MY TIME AIN'T LONG**

*The cotton field.*

*Large, bright harvest moon overhead.*

GRANDFATHER *wears a cotton sack. He gives another to* SON.

MOTHER *picks cotton nearby.*

GRANDFATHER. Don't just stand there like time on
    a monument. Get to work.

SON. I don't know how.

GRANDFATHER. It's easy enough. It's in your blood.

   GRANDFATHER *demonstrates.*

   This here the stalk. This here the boll. When this boll get
   good and ready, and not a second before, it'll open up and
   there: King Cotton.

*He pulls off a lock of cotton.*

SON *follows his example.*

   Be careful now –

SON. Ouch!

GRANDFATHER. That's the burr. They prick a little at first.
    But you'll have a callus 'fore long.

SON. How much cotton you think I can pick, Grandfather?

GRANDFATHER. Well, I picked five hundred pounds in a day
    once, Son. But that's when I was a young man. I was 'bout
    your age, but I was built.

MOTHER. And ask him how much he made for the five
    hundred pounds of cotton he picked.

SON. How much did you make, Grandfather?

GRANDFATHER. Ten             MOTHER. Ten dollars.
    dollars.

SON. Mother, you've heard this story before?

MOTHER. Surprised you made it this long without hearing it, Son.

GRANDFATHER. Five hundred pure pounds of white gold in one twenty-four-hour time span. And there wasn't a burr or leaf or a twig in the lot. Some fellas used to take and put stones in they bag to make it weigh out more. But I took pride in my work. No gettin' over for me – Now, pay attention to what you doin'. You leavin' cotton in that burr. That's leaving money on the vine.

SON. How you get it to come out so clean?

GRANDFATHER. Practice.     MOTHER. Practice.

SON. Wouldn't it be easier to just take the whole thing off? I hear they have machines that can separate them now.

GRANDFATHER. That's the problem with folks nowadays. Think everything oughta be controlled by a button. You gon' learn to do it like I say or you'll be up all night cow-lickin'.

SON. Cow-lickin'? What's that?

MOTHER. That's when you spread out the burrs and the seeds in front of a fire. Easier to get the stray fibers out when they hot.

SON. I'd rather do that, than to be out here all night.

GRANDFATHER. Nonsense. Cotton pickin' by the harvest moon? Moonlight just as bright as the sun. Remind me of them cotton-pickin' days when I was a youngster. Folks used to say they was just as good as them cotton-pickin' days before the war. It was a big to-do. Everybody helpin' everybody else. We all had cotton to pick so we made a party out of it. Negros can make a party out of anything. We pick one field, fast, 'cause we was all workin' together. And we a-move on to the next. And we didn't quit workin' till every field was picked clean. But there was lots of food to be ate and liquor to be drunk. Used to be a prize for the person who picked the most. I won with them five hundred pounds. Beat out that pretty boy, Willie Lavender, who up to that point held the record for most cotton picked in a day. And he was almos' twice my size.

SON. What did you win, Grandfather?

GRANDFATHER. A jug of moonshine. My daddy 'llowed me to drank it too. He say if I work as good as a man, I oughta be able to drink as good as one. I was proud. Still am. I out-picked grown men. And that night I got drunk like a man. And I danced. And I sang them songs we always sang.

SON. So let's make a deal. If I pick more than you, I can have a swig of that whiskey you keep under the bathroom sink.

MOTHER. No deal.

SON. Mother –

GRANDFATHER. Pick five hundred pounds and then we'll talk.

GRANDFATHER, MOTHER *and* SON *pick cotton by the harvest moon.*

GRANDFATHER *begins to hum. His humming soon becomes a song. As he sings their picking keeps time with the music.*

I feel like, I feel like, Lord,
I feel like my time ain't long;
I feel like, I feel like, Lord,
I feel like my time ain't long.
Saw death in the mirr' the other day.

MOTHER. I feel like my time ain't long.

GRANDFATHER. Won't leave me 'lone, won't go away.

MOTHER. I feel like my time ain't long.

BOTH. I feel like, I feel like, Lord,
I feel like my time ain't long;
I feel like, I feel like, Lord,
I feel like my time ain't long;

GRANDFATHER. Can see heaven's gate from my front do'.

GRANDFATHER *gestures for* SON *to fill in the blank.*

SON. I feel like my time ain't long?

GRANDFATHER. Just like Br'er Cotton, cain't take it no mo'.

MOTHER. I feel like my time ain't long.

GRANDFATHER. Gonna put all my toilin' and burdens down.

BOTH. I feel like my time ain't long.

GRANDFATHER. Listenin' fo' da glory trumpets sound.

BOTH. I feel like my time ain't long.

ALL. I feel like, I feel like, Lord,
  I feel like my time ain't long;
  I feel like, I feel like, Lord,
  I feel like my time ain't long.

  *The chorus is repeated as the trio picks cotton by the moonlight.*

**MORNING**

*The kitchen / cotton field.*

*The cotton field has grown further into the kitchen. Vines and cotton stalks abound.*

*A large oak tree has grown in the middle of the kitchen, overturning the table and chairs.*

RUFFRINO *and* NADINE *enter, they are both dressed in funeral blacks.*

NADINE. You hungry?

> RUFFRINO *marvels at the tree. He alone can see it.*

RUFFRINO. Naw.

NADINE. Sister from the church brought over a casserole. I can warm that up?

RUFFRINO. I'm good.

> NADINE *notices the table. She moves it.*
>
> *She moves the chairs. She considers all.*

NADINE. It was a nice service.

RUFFRINO. Nobody was there.

NADINE. There was folks there.

RUFFRINO. Not enough. Not for as old as he was.

NADINE. It was a nice service.

RUFFRINO. It was a waste of money, that's what it was.

NADINE. What's it to you? That's how come I work every day. To pay for stuff like this.

RUFFRINO....

NADINE. Speaking of which... I picked up a extra shift tonight. You gon' be alright here by yourself?

RUFFRINO. You going to work? Today? You leavin' me –

NADINE. I got to.

RUFFRINO. We didn't need such a fancy box. We should have put his ass in a Space Bag and called it a damn day.

NADINE. Hush now! It ain't right to speak ill of the dead.

RUFFRINO. So just 'cause he dead I'm supposed to forget that he was spineless old fool. You know the day he died –

NADINE. And I'm glad I made you stay home that day. Least he wasn't by himself.

RUFFRINO. He shoulda died by himself. He was a weak-ass old coward and I wish I had never found it out.

NADINE. What are you talkin'about?

RUFFRINO. He said Witherspoons ain't remarkable. There's nothing special about us.

NADINE. You gotta understand. Matthew comes from a different time –

RUFFRINO. It's probably true though. I mean he wasn't shit. And you… You so nothin' you can't even afford to take a day off cleaning some white man's toilet to mourn your own not-shit father –

NADINE. RUFFRINO! I know you mad and you grieving. But you need to stop!

RUFFRINO. He really had me believing that I was destined to be a nobody too. Just like y'all. But then I remembered: I'm not really a Witherspoon. I mean if you had done things right I woulda been a Fleming like my father. But of course you fucked that up too –

NADINE *slaps him.*

…

RUFFRINO *sits down in front of the TV.*

*He turns on the Xbox and picks up the controller.*

NADINE. Ruffrino?

*He ignores her.*

Ruffrino I…

RUFFRINO....

NADINE. I gotta get ready for work.

RUFFRINO *plays the Xbox.*

Don't sit here and play that damn game all day.

RUFFRINO *plays the Xbox.*

Right.

NADINE *exits.*

*The kitchen sinks several inches deeper.*

RUFFRINO *discovers another cotton plant growing under his seat.*

**NADINE WEEPS**

*Another room in another home. Or at least the suggestion of one.*

NADINE *cleans.*

NADINE....

   NADINE *cleans.*

   ...

   NADINE *cleans.*

   ...

   NADINE *breaks.*

   NADINE *weeps.*

   NADINE *weeps.*

   NADINE *weeps.*

   OFFICER *enters.*

   NADINE *hides her weeping.*

OFFICER. Well, if it isn't Nadine Maurice Witherspoon.

NADINE. You figured out my name.

OFFICER. Name, address, date of birth, Social Security...
   You'd be surprised how much information you can get when
   you flash a badge.

   *He sees her tears.*

   You're crying. I'm sorry –

NADINE. For what? You ain't done nothin'.

OFFICER. I'm sorry. I see a woman crying, I apologize. It's
   a reflex.

NADINE. Oh.

OFFICER. But I do owe you an apology actually –

NADINE. No. I owe you one. I was rude.

OFFICER. I was rude first. I shouldn't have called you pathetic. Or told you to give up hope. I was miserable. Still am actually. And I guess I wanted company. My shrink calls it emotional contagion. I'm really sorry –

NADINE. I buried my father this morning. Plot 482. Fort Hills Memorial Park.

OFFICER. Are you serious?

NADINE. Yeah. How's that for 'emotional contagion'?

OFFICER. What are you doing here? You should be at home with your family.

NADINE. I can't afford to grieve.

OFFICER. I am so sorry –

NADINE. Stop sayin' you sorry to me.

OFFICER. I'm sorry – Sorry! Sorry –

NADINE. I thought I wanted to be a nurse for him. To make him proud. But I can see now, I was doing it out of spite. I can tell 'cause I ain't got that pit in my stomach no more. Ya know? It was all this anger and resentment towards him that was driving me, 'cause he had such a low opinion of his daughter. Then he went and died thinking he was right about me.

*Pregnant silence.*

OFFICER. So... since you told me to stop apologizing, I'm sorta at a loss for what to say. But I know I should say something. What do you want me to say?

NADINE. You could ask me how I feel. Don't nobody ever ask me how I feel.

OFFICER. Okay. How do you feel, Nadine?

NADINE. Honestly? In this moment, I feel... relief. I got nobody's expectations or disappointments to live up to no more.

OFFICER. Silver lining I guess? What about your son? I'm sure he's proud of you, for not giving up. For trying again –

NADINE. He don't know. Nobody knows. I figured I wouldn't tell nobody, so if and when I quit they wouldn't think any less of me.

OFFICER. So how is your son taking all this?

NADINE. Like he take everything else: personally.

OFFICER. Could you tell me about him.

NADINE *smiles*.

NADINE. He's a mess. He's fourteen. He'll be fifteen in June. Ruffrino is his name. He's brilliant. Maybe a little too brilliant. And he's scared. All the time. Every day. And he acts up to mask it, the fear, but a mother sees.

OFFICER. So what does his father do about it?

NADINE. He sends him Black Panther books from jail.

OFFICER. Maybe I could talk to him –

NADINE. That's a terrible idea.

OFFICER. Maybe he should talk to a professional. Both of you really. When my wife left me it really helped to confide in someone –

NADINE. I can't afford to confide.

OFFICER. Maybe your pastor could –

NADINE. Look, you don't have to try and fix my problems. My woes ain't got nothin' to do with you.

OFFICER. I can't help it. When I see a woman in distress I have to try and fix it. It's a reflex.

NADINE. But –

OFFICER *hugs her*. NADINE *lets go. She weeps and weeps and weeps until:*

*She laughs and laughs and cries and laughs –*

OFFICER. What's so funny?

NADINE. Nothin'. It's just you know so much about me. More than anybody else. I think that make you like... my best friend.

*They laugh together.*

OFFICER. Why don't you take the rest of the day off?

NADINE. I can't –

OFFICER. Listen to your BFF. Go be with your son. You two need each other. Now more than ever.

OFFICER *scribbles on a piece of paper.*

This is my number. If you need anything. Anything at all, day or night, I'm just a phone call away.

NADINE *takes the paper.*

NADINE. Maybe they did teach you something about being noble after all.

## DIASPORA II

*A post-apocalyptic wasteland, or at least the suggestion of one.*

RUFFRINO *and* CAGED_BIRD99 *wear their armor.*

CAGED_BIRD99. Look alert! There's a couple of zalien scouts on my radar.

RUFFRINO....

RUFFRINO *runs forward shooting aimlessly.*

CAGED_BIRD99. RuffandRino look out!

*An ax slices into* RUFFRINO*'s armor. He drops to the ground.*

*PROJECTION: 'RUFFandRINO has been slaughtered'.*

CAGED_BIRD99 *waits.*

RUFFRINO....

CAGED_BIRD99....

RUFFRINO *respawns.*

Br'er. What's up with you today? It's like you're trying to get killed.

RUFFRINO. Shut up and play the game.

CAGED_BIRD99....

Is something wrong?

RUFFRINO. No.

CAGED_BIRD99. It sure seems like there's –

RUFFRINO. Let's just play the game. Alright?

CAGED_BIRD99. Fine.

RUFFRINO. Fine.

CAGED_BIRD99. We've cleared this quadrant. Let's move on to quadrant four, the enemies are harder but there's more XP –

*Suddenly: the whisper of a sniper's bullet.*

CAGED_BIRD99 *collapses to the ground silently.*

RUFFRINO. The fuck?

*PROJECTION: 'CAGED_BIRD99 has been sniped by redneck_swag'.*

Not this shit again.

RUFFRINO *takes cover.*

Why don't you come out you asshole? You a man or nah?

*Several more of the sniper's bullets are heard. They miss.*

Missed me you fucktard. Quit sniping like a little bitch –

*Suddenly we hear the approach of a missile. Followed by a loud explosion!*

RUFFRINO *is blown back!*

*PROJECTION: 'RUFFandRINO has been blown to smithereens by redneck_swag'.*

*redneck_swag cackles with glee.*

REDNECK_SWAG. DIE YOU FUCKING RETARD NIGGERS DIE!! FUCK YOU NIGGERS!! FUCK YOU NIGGERS!! BURN! BUUURRRRNN! BOW DOWN TO YOUR MASTER! BOW DOWN TO YOU MASTER YOU FUCKING FAGGOT NIGGERS!

*PROJECTION: 'redneck_swag has logged off'.*

CAGED_BIRD99 *respawns.*

RUFFRINO *respawns.*

RUFFRINO. FUUUUCCCKK!!

RUFFRINO *begins firing rounds aimlessly.*

CAGED_BIRD99. Dude. Be careful. I've got friendly fire turned on.

RUFFRINO. Who gives a fuck about this game?

CAGED_BIRD99. You love this game.

RUFFRINO. I hate this shit! I hate all of it!

CAGED_BIRD99. Well they just announced *Diaspora II*'s coming out –

RUFFRINO. Not the fuckin' game – Life! The world! My fuckin' family! I hate all this shit!

CAGED_BIRD99. That sounds like your rage again. You should count –

RUFFRINO. Fuck counting!

CAGED_BIRD99. Why do you let redneck_swag get to you? He's just some loser kid.

RUFFRINO. It's not just him. It's what he stands for.

CAGED_BIRD99. Which is?

RUFFRINO. The corrosive majority perception that 'other' somehow means 'less than'.

CAGED_BIRD99. I understand that. Believe me, I do, but –

RUFFRINO. I can't even play a fucking game without being reminded that I'm just some 'nigger'. That fuckin' word, man! Why the fuck should he call me that? Why?! And I can't do nothing to protect myself from it, there's no weapon to combat that shit. There's no armor I can put on against it. At any moment I can be a 'nigger'. At any moment I can be 'less than' just because some white muthafucka says so. No matter where I am, no matter what I do, at any moment I can be just some worthless 'nigger'. THAT FUCKING WORD!

CAGED_BIRD99. He's just a loser kid sitting in a trailer somewhere drinking a Super Gulp of Mountain Dew. He doesn't matter.

RUFFRINO. But loser kids like him grow and kill black kids like us. And they get away with it. I wish I could just crack his head open and find the thing in his brain that makes him racist and pulverize it. But I can't! I'm starting to see that I can't change nothin'. I can't change nobody.

CAGED_BIRD99. Maya Angelou said: If you can't change something, change your attitude –

RUFFRINO. I HATE WHITE PEOPLE!

CAGED_BIRD99. How is that helpful?

RUFFRINO. What are you talking about?

CAGED_BIRD99. Hating back. You can't fight hate with hate.

RUFFRINO. Why the hell not?

CAGED_BIRD99. An eye for an eye makes the whole world blind. That's Gandhi.

RUFFRINO. How 'bout, you take my eye, I fuckin' decapitate you. That's Ruffrino.

CAGED_BIRD99. I –

RUFFRINO. The verdict came back today on the D'Wayne Chambers case up in Charlottesville.

CAGED_BIRD99. I heard. No charges.

RUFFRINO. Can you believe that? You would think at this point, with all the backlash these cases are getting that they would've charged him out of guilt. Or to appease us. To set an example. But they setting the example they want to set. That black people don't matter and they're willing to show us this over and over and over and over and over –

CAGED_BIRD99. I'm sorry –

RUFFRINO. Don't say sorry to me. That's what those privileged crackers say to me at school. 'I'm sorry.' They feel sorry for me. Like it's my problem. Like it's my issue. Like it doesn't affect them. But then they don't have to fear being shot down by the police. So… I'm done. I've done the peaceful protests and the silent vigils. It's time-out for peaceful. They need to feel it.

CAGED_BIRD99. What does that mean? You're scaring me, br'er. I've never heard you talk like this. Is there something else going on?

RUFFRINO. What the fuck ELSE needs to be going on? Other than WHAT THE FUCK IS GOING ON!

CAGED_BIRD99. I just –

RUFFRINO. You know, I thought you got it. I thought you understood me. But I'm starting to think you just as 'sleep as the rest of the zombies.

CAGED_BIRD99. RuffandRino –

RUFFRINO. Get at me when you wake the hell up! –

*PROJECTION: 'RUFFandRINO has logged off'.*

CAGED_BIRD99 *is left alone in game.*

(*Slam poetry.*)

CAGED_BIRD99. We meet over distance and difference
Yet they name us just the same
Our word for acceptance is right on the tip our tongues
It's… It's… It's…
Our vocabulary fails us
But we have many words for lonely
As many as the Eskimos for snow.
We're both forsaken, you and I
But we understand each other
and our language of the misunderstood

## AN ACORN

*The kitchen / cotton field.*

RUFFRINO *sits a the dinner table, rummaging through boxes of old keepsakes and bric-à-brac.*

*He discovers a picture of* MATTHEW. *He stares at it a little too long.*

*A breeze stirs the leaves of the tree.*

RUFFRINO....

*A breeze still.*

Matthew?

*In response, an acorn falls from the tree and lands on the table.*

RUFFRINO *marvels at it.*

*Another acorn falls from the tree. It rains acorns. Another. And then another.*

*Another.*

*And then... a Space Bag.*

RUFFRINO *retrieves the bag. He cuts into it with a knife.*

*He removes a pair of pants and then a Confederate soldier's hat. He places the hat atop his head for safe keeping.*

*He removes a jacket. In the inside pocket he finds bolls of cotton. He marvels at them.*

*He keeps digging. And then: money.*

*Enough money to change their lives.*

Crazy-ass fool...

*Just then* NADINE *can be heard entering the house.*

RUFFRINO *hastily shoves the money and the uniform back into the Space Bag and, thinking quickly, he stashes it under the kitchen sink.*

*As* NADINE *enters,* RUFFRINO *realizes he is still wearing the cap. He ducks under the table and stashes the hat.*

NADINE *wasn't expecting to see* RUFFRINO, *she's still holding her school books.*

*She doubles back to hide them.*

*They both miss what the other is hiding.*

NADINE *re-enters.*

NADINE. Why're you under the table?

RUFFRINO. Why do you keep moving the furniture? Everything we got is trash, don't matter where it is.

NADINE. You know who you sound like don't you?

RUFFRINO....

NADINE. You hungry? I picked up some Cheesies.

*She holds up an oily brown-paper bag.*

RUFFRINO. How come you home so early?

NADINE. I wanted to be here. With you.

RUFFRINO. All of a sudden.

NADINE. No not all of a sudden – Please Ruffrino. I don't want to fight.

*She surveys the room.*

What is all this mess?

RUFFRINO. Matthew's shit.

NADINE *cuts her eyes.*

Stuff. Matthew's stuff.

NADINE. He was a hoarder and I ain't even know it. Huh. What are you doing with it?

RUFFRINO. Nothing. Looking I guess.

NADINE. Looking for what? His buried treasure?

RUFFRINO. No.

NADINE. I hate to break it to you, but you ain't gon' find nothin' valuable. Unless you know somebody interested in old receipts and bits of paper.

RUFFRINO. And obituaries. That's why nobody was at his funeral. All his friend are dead people.

NADINE. It's sad really. A man live sixty-some odd years and what he got to show for it? Bills! Bills he still ain't paid. Bills somebody else gon' have to pay.

RUFFRINO. I thought we shouldn't speak ill of the dead.

NADINE. It ain't about speaking ill. It's the truth. Promise me this, Ruffrino. I don't care where you go or what you do with your life, just promise me you won't be the type of man to make a mess and walk away. Promise me that.

RUFFRINO. Can I get one of them Cheesies?

NADINE. Here. You want me to nuke it?

RUFFRINO. No. I like 'em cold.

NADINE. Nasty. You gon' get sick.

RUFFRINO. What? Is that your medical opinion?

NADINE *considers this*.

NADINE. I don't know what kind of opinion it is.

RUFFRINO....

NADINE. Eat.

RUFFRINO *unwraps and eats a burger.*

NADINE *watches him.*

This is nice. Us. Talking like civilized people. Sharing a meal, no fighting no –

RUFFRINO *cuts her off by turning on the TV.*

*They watch.*

RUFFRINO *eats*. NADINE *watches him*.

NADINE *watches TV*. RUFFRINO *watches her*.

What – What are you looking at?

RUFFRINO. I never noticed how old you are. When I'm just
thinking about you, in my mind, you're real young and
pretty. But just now, in this light, in that chair right here in
this kitchen, you look old... and cracked.

NADINE. Gee. Thanks.

*Something on TV catches her attention.*

Hold on now, turn that up... What in the world is going on in
this world?

*The sounds of protests and rioting emanate from the TV.*

RUFFRINO. That's Charlottesville!

NADINE. Oh my stars. That is Charlottesville. Looks like
a third-world country.

RUFFRINO. This is                NADINE. This is terrible.
awesome!

NADINE. Awesome? What could possibly be awesome about
this.

RUFFRINO. Finally somebody's doing something. They
standing up. They fighting back!

NADINE. By tearing up they own neighborhoods, looting,
starting fires in they own streets –

RUFFRINO. What they neighborhoods ever done for them?
What the streets ever done for them? I gotta get to
Charlottesville!

NADINE. Excuse me?

RUFFRINO. I need to be there. This is my moment. The
revolution is being televised. It's my time to wake
everybody up!

NADINE. You a fool if you think I'm 'bout to let you go get involved in that mess.

RUFFRINO. You a fool if you think you can stop me.

NADINE. How you gon' get there?

RUFFRINO. I'll take the Greyhound.

NADINE. If you can afford a Greyhound you should be able to put some money on some of these bills we got around here.

RUFFRINO. Is that all you think about? Bills?

NADINE. When you ain't got the money to pay the bills, it tend to be the first thing on your mind.

RUFFRINO. Some things are bigger than bills, Nadine.

NADINE. I wouldn't know. Now you ain't going to no Charlottesville! They causin' enough trouble on they own. What good you gon' do being just another monkey in the crowd?

RUFFRINO. I'm going.

NADINE. You ain't!

RUFFRINO. Try and stop me.

*They face off.*

RUFFRINO *attempts to push past* NADINE.

NADINE *grabs* RUFFRINO *by the shirt. She begins to hit him about the head and shoulders. Each word is punctuated by punch or a slap.*

| NADINE. You. Ain't. Going. Nowhere. | RUFFRINO. Get off of me! Let me go! |
|---|---|
| What's. Wrong. With. You? | Stop! |
| You. Trying. To. Get. | Stop! |
| Killed! Huh! You. Wanna. Go. To. Jail? | STOP! |
| | STOP! |

RUFFRINO *is finally able break free of* NADINE.

RUFFRINO. FUUUCKK!! Wake up Nadine! There's scarier things than jail! There's bigger shit than death!

*He storms out. Slams the door!*

*The kitchen sinks; down, down and down.*

*Vines and cotton stalks push out of every crack and crevice.*

*The cotton field encroaches deeper into the house.*

NADINE *is exhausted and weeping.*

RUFFRINO *exits.*

NADINE *doesn't object.*

**NADINE WAITS**

NADINE *sits waiting.*

*As she waits the cotton field overtakes the house. It over grows her. Vines and stalks of cotton root her to the chair.*

*Yet* NADINE *waits.*

*Moonlight gives way to sunrise, then morning.*

NADINE *picks up the phone. She dials the number from the piece of paper.*

NADINE. Hey, um… Officer… I just realized I don't even know your name. Which makes this crazy. This is crazy. It's so early. I don't know why I'm calling… Well I do. But I don't think that I should be. You're kind of a stranger. But I'm worried about Ruffrino, my son. We had a big fight, and he been gone all night. I think he might be in some kinda trouble. I just got this feelin' of impending disaster. Like it's lurking 'round in the furrows. And more so than usual. And it feels like I been here before. I know I have actually. And just like then, I can't move. Stuck in this rut. 'Cause the past ain't no great comfort. And the future don't seem to be offerin' no solace. I'm not calling because I want you to do anything. It's my problem. Really. I just wanted someone to listen. I guess your voicemail will have to do for the moment –

RUFFRINO *returns.*

NADINE *hangs up the phone.*

You back.

RUFFRINO. I need to prepare.

NADINE. Prepare for what?

RUFFRINO. War.

NADINE. I hate to break it to you, but you ain't going to no war –

RUFFRINO. I'm going to Charlottesville, Nadine and you can't stop me –

NADINE. I know about the money.

RUFFRINO. You found –

NADINE. The eighty-three dollars and eleven cents you had hid under your bed.

RUFFRINO. Oh. That money.

NADINE. I spent it.

RUFFRINO. You what?

NADINE. At least I'm going to. I'm going right down to Appalachian Power and putting that money on the light bill. So there, you ain't got no money for no Greyhound no more.

RUFFRINO. Then I'll walk if I have to.

NADINE. Ruffrino –

RUFFRINO. You so damn 'sleep! You really think money is gonna stop me from doing what I need to do? I ain't you.

NADINE. I been sittin' here all night. Thinking. 'Bout you. 'Bout my life. 'Bout this family. I feel like I turned gray overnight. We hangin' on by a thread. Danglin'. And the only thing that can save us, the only thing that can get us on solid ground again is you. I need you to save us, Ruffrino –

RUFFRINO. That's what I'm trying to do! I'm trying to save the world, Nadine! For us! Don't you understand that?

NADINE *uproots herself from the chair.*

*She faces off with* RUFFRINO.

RUFFRINO *braces himself.*

NADINE *reaches out… and embraces him.*

RUFFRINO *resists.*

*But she holds on to him.*

NADINE. I don't wanna fight with you no more. I can't.

NADINE *holds on to him. He lets go, he finds comfort in her arms.*

You becomin' a man. And I can't make your decisions for you.

RUFFRINO….

NADINE. You remindin' me of your father right now. He was afraid too once. And he stood right where you standing. Between one decision and another. And I couldn't do nothin' then either. So I tol' him the same thing I'ma tell you: Make the right choice.

*NADINE gives RUFFRINO back his bookbag.*

*She begins to exit.*

RUFFRINO. Where are you going?

NADINE. Where I'm always going. To work.

*She exits.*

*RUFFRINO is torn with indecision. He teeters from one notion to the next.*

*He gathers the money and the uniform from under the sink and places all on the table.*

*He considers. He paces.*

*He turns on the Xbox. Picks up the controller.*

*He's transported to the world of* Diaspora.

RUFFRINO. Cagedbird! Cagedbird!

*PROJECTION: 'CAGED_BIRD99 is offline'.*

I'm sorry. I need you. Please! I need your help. You're the only one who understands! I need you...

*RUFFRINO breaks.*

I need you.

*PROJECTION: 'CAGED_BIRD99 has logged on'.*

CAGED_BIRD99. Hey... Sorry. I was on invisible mode, redneck_swagg was trolling me again.

RUFFRINO. Guess where I'm headed?

CAGED_BIRD99. To school. What time is it where you are?

RUFFRINO. I don't know. Early. Guess again.

CAGED_BIRD99. I don't know, just tell me.

RUFFRINO. Charlottesville.

CAGED_BIRD99. Virginia?

RUFFRINO. Yes.

CAGED_BIRD99. They're rioting in Charlottesville. Aren't they? It's all over the news. Why would you wanna go there?

RUFFRINO. You just answered your own question.

CAGED_BIRD99. It looks dangerous.

RUFFRINO. The world is dangerous, Cagedbird. And if the white man is gonna continue to use violence against us at some point we should start using it back. If they kill us –

CAGED_BIRD99. Then what? You kill them?

RUFFRINO. Maybe. Maybe then they'll pay attention. I'm sick of it being my issue. I'm tired of white people hurting us. I'm tired of white people killing us and getting away with it! I FUCKING HATE WHITE PEOPLE –

CAGED_BIRD99. I'M WHITE!

RUFFRINO. What? What do you mean?

CAGED_BIRD99. I'm... white. And that's a weird thing for me to say. I don't think I've ever said it before because it's never mattered before. Because so much of me, my identity is CP. That's cerebral palsy, which is a little like a stroke that happens when you're born...

RUFFRINO. Cagedbird, what the fuck are you talking about?

CAGED_BIRD99. Since I can remember I've always described myself in those terms. 'Cerebral palsy, which is a little like a stroke that happens when you're born.' In terms of my condition. So being white was never an issue.

RUFFRINO. So then why didn't you tell me?

CAGED_BIRD99. Because. I was just happy to find a friend who didn't see me as broken. Because that's how I see myself, and that's how you see yourself. And we bonded over that. Because I know what it's like to be judged by sight alone. To have to make excuses for being born the way you were born.

RUFFRINO. So you think being black is the same as being a retard.

CAGED_BIRD99. That's so ugly. That's not you talking.

RUFFRINO. How do you know? You don't know who I am, 'cause apparently I don't know who the fuck you are.

CAGED_BIRD99. I know you're better than that. I know you know me. You actually see me. I know I don't understand your struggle completely... I never could. Or you mine for that matter. But we speak the same language you and I –

RUFFRINO. The fuck we do. I speak the truth and you're a fuckin' liar.

CAGED_BIRD99. I'm sorry –

RUFFRINO. You betrayed me –

CAGED_BIRD99. I'm sorry.

RUFFRINO. Don't say sorry to me!

RUFFRINO *seethes*. CAGED_BIRD99 *shrinks*.

CAGED_BIRD99....

RUFFRINO....

CAGED_BIRD99. Do you hate me now?

RUFFRINO. Yeah...

But not because you're white.

*PROJECTION: 'RuffandRino has logged off'.*

CAGED_BIRD99 *is left alone in game.*

*She breaks.*

(*Slam poetry.*)

CAGED_BIRD99. We meet over pain and loss
Pain of judgement and anger at the loss
The loss of nothing; yet missing something

Frustration because we're not quite sure what
And the words build into a tidal wave
That breaks upon the shore
And it breaks us and erodes us
It strips us, you and I
But we understand each other
And our language of the festering

*Simultaneously:*

RUFFRINO *takes the items from the Space Bag. He puts on the Confederate uniform.*

*As he puts on the jacket, he discovers several bullet holes in it.*

*As he places the hat atop his head, the final piece, the kitchen begins to sink gravely. Down and down and down.*

*The kitchen is overwelmed by the cotton field. The cotton field has taken back the house.*

*The leaves on the oak tree begin to stir.*

RUFFRINO *removes the ax from his bookbag.*

*He begins to chop down the tree. It's a small ax and a big tree and as he chops his anger and rage and frustrations grows like vines.*

RUFFRINO *chops.*

RUFFRINO....

RUFFRINO *chops.*

...

RUFFRINO *chops.*

...

*Suddenly* OFFICER *enters.*

OFFICER. Hello? Hello? I'm looking for Nadine Witherspoon –

RUFFRINO *freezes. He holds the ax up.*

Ruffrino?

RUFFRINO *sees red. He attacks the officer with the ax.*

*They struggle over the ax.*

*They wrestle.*

*They wrestle.*

*They wrestle.*

*They wrestle.*

*Until,* RUFFRINO *takes the* OFFICER*'s gun.*

*He aims the gun at* OFFICER.

OFFICER *puts his hands up.*

Listen. Kid. Don't shoot.

RUFFRINO....

OFFICER. Look. My hands are up. Don't shoot.

I don't know what's going on here, but... you don't have to do this.

RUFFRINO....

OFFICER. I'm a friend. I'm a friend of your mother. She cleans my house –

RUFFRINO *clicks off the safety and concentrates his aim.*

RUFFRINO....

OFFICER. Listen. I'm here because she called me. She said she was worried about you –

RUFFRINO. Shut up!

OFFICER. Ruffrino!

RUFFRINO. Stop saying my name!

OFFICER. I'm a friend of your mom. My name is –

RUFFRINO. I don't want to know your name!

OFFICER. Don't do this. Please, Ruff–

RUFFRINO. Stop saying my fuckin' name!

OFFICER. Look, don't do this to your mom. Okay? She's been through enough.

RUFFRINO. What do you know about it?

OFFICER. We're friends. We talk. Hey, I bet you didn't know she was back in college.

RUFFRINO. That's a lie!

OFFICER. No. She's studying to be a nurse. A baby nurse. She's been taking night-school classes – She doesn't need this. You don't need this. Just put the gun down, I'm sure we can get this all figured out.

RUFFRINO. No! NO! It doesn't matter... I see it now. I don't need to go to Charlottesville. The revolution starts right here! Right now! With us. Men like you are shooting kids like me, every day –

OFFICER. I haven't shot anybody!

RUFFRINO. But white men just like you are shooting black kids just like me, every day AND GETTING AWAY WITH IT!

OFFICER. I'm not a villain here, kid. Hell, I'm not even a hero. I'm not the problem –

RUFFRINO. Yeah... but you look like it.

RUFFRINO *fires the gun.*

*The faces of slaughtered black boys flash across his mind.*

*He fires again.*

*And then again.*

*And again. And again.*

*Blackout.*

**EPILOGUE**

*The cotton field.*

MOTHER, *a new mother, cradling an infant. Timeless.*

*This is a lullaby.* MOTHER *fills the beats (…) with song.*

MOTHER. Everyone was glad to live in such close proximity to heaven, it made them content to have heaven's front door be in rock-skippin' distance. But being so close and yet so far away kept Br'er Cotton tossing and turning at nights.

…

'Why,' he thought. 'Why can I only enjoy heaven in my dreams?'

…

The unfairness of it all infuriated Br'er Cotton to the point where he grew stones in his stomach. Till this one day, no special day in particular, save it was the day that he finally made his decision. On this very ordinary day Br'er Cotton decided he could take it no longer. He was gonna break into heaven.

…

…

*End of play.*

**A Nick Hern Book**

*Br'er Cotton* first published in Great Britain in 2018 as a paperback original by Nick Hern Books Limited, The Glasshouse, 49a Goldhawk Road, London W12 8QP, in association with Theatre503, London

*Br'er Cotton* © 2018 Tearrance Arvelle Chisholm

Tearrance Arvelle Chisholm has asserted his moral right to be identified as the author of this work

Cover photography by Graham Michael. Cover design by Rebecca Pitt.

Designed and typeset by Nick Hern Books, London
Printed in Great Britain by Mimeo Ltd, Huntingdon, Cambridgeshire PE29 6XX

A CIP catalogue record for this book is available from the British Library

ISBN 978 1 84842 752 5